RIDE THE JACK RABBIT

MORE OF THE PEOPLE, PLACES, AND EVENTS THAT MAKE MICHIANA FASCINATING

AARON HELMAN

*All photos and reproductions are taken from the public domain
or collection of the author, unless otherwise noted.*

To S.B.
Forever and always.

Where the tall grasses nod at the close of the day
And the sycamore's shadow is slanting away-
Where the whip-poor-will chants from a far distant limb
Just as if the whole business was all made for him.
Oh! It's now that my thoughts, flying back on the wings
Of the rail and he die-away song that he sings,
Brings the tears to my eyes that drip off into rhyme,
And I live once again in the old summer time;
For my soul it seems caught in old time's under-tow
And I'm floating away down the river St. Joe.

- Ben King (1857-1894)

CHAPTER ONE

RIDE THE JACK RABBIT

My wife and I began our walk in August of 2022, just a few weeks after a bout with Covid robbed me of the vitality that had taken me two years to regain, and at the exact spot where an affable Alabamian named Tim Flock sailed beneath a riffling checkered flag to claim the win in the only NASCAR race ever staged in South Bend, Indiana. The half-mile dirt track is long gone, replaced once by a nine-hole golf course, and then by a parking lot beneath a complex of student apartments that are themselves fading into various states of disrepair. Like it does anywhere else, time marches on, in defiance or forgetfulness of every important thing that has ever happened. A fenced-off concrete grandstand is all that remains of the Playland Park Speedway, where in 1952, some 3,700 boisterous fans cheered Flock to victory.

Tim Flock's visit to South Bend came amidst the greatest streak of success in his entire career, a stretch that saw him win seven of eleven consecutive races and finish second three more times. The race in South Bend was marred by a wreck when a driver from nearby Muncie flipped his Studebaker. Able-bodied fans were recruited from the grandstands to help push the thing upright again, but luckily, no one was seriously injured and Flock's victory counted just the same. By the end of the season, he would be crowned NASCAR's champion for the first time in his career. He won that title driving The Fabulous Hudson Hornet, perhaps the most storied and nostalgic race car of all time, one later remembered and returned to fame in the Pixar film, *Cars*. The Hudson Hornet in that movie is a crotchety old timer named Doc

1

Hudson who lambastes the younger and cockier Lightning McQueen for his own insistence on egoism and showmanship.

Turns out, Doc Hudson might not have been a fan of Tim Flock either.

Flock's success in the 1952 season led him to some truly peculiar fame-seeking and celebrity-indulgent behaviors. In fact, by 1953, during actual sanctioned NASCAR races, Flock adopted the bizarre strategy of employing a co-pilot in his car, a rhesus monkey named Jocko Flocko. The monkey had his own goggles, helmet, and racing uniform; and in spring of 1953, Jocko Flocko would experience his greatest success. Nearly a year after Tim Flock's performance at Playland Park, his primate passenger was present on pole position for a race in Hickory, North Carolina that the duo would win, another of Flock's 39 career victories. To this day, Jocko Flocko remains the only monkey winner of a NASCAR race. However, things began to unravel a few weeks later on a racetrack in Raleigh when the bored monkey, to Flock's shock and horror, began pushing buttons and pulling levers inside the car. Jocko Flocko ended up costing his driver the win that day and was retired unceremoniously shortly thereafter.

It is with no small amount of disappointment that I relay to you that the monkey was not present with Flock during his victory in South Bend, a day that exists only as a hazy memory filled in by a blurry image discovered in a chilled microfilm room, one of the only remaining remnants of the high point of the Playland Park Speedway, the other being the concrete bleachers that are more reminiscent of a dystopian movie set than a place that was once a fine destination for tens of thousands of visitors every summer for the better part of a century.

It all started as a leisure stop along the Northern Indiana Railway, a place where passengers could pause for a picnic, some fresh air, and a view of the river. After the railroad company added a few simple rides to entertain families and to generate a little bit of extra revenue, the place was given its first name – Springbrook Park. Recognizing that the place had more potential as a day trip destination than a brief whistle stop, a man named Charles Deibel leased the property from the railroad and hired Earl Redden to run it. By 1925, the place was a success, Redden bought the land outright, renamed the place Playland Park, and built an amusement facility that would become the pride of the city.

Redden was a natural showman and kept ad revenue flowing into newspapers' coffers on an almost daily basis. He sought national acts and national celebrities and invented new reasons for families to come back to Playland Park again and again. Horse racing, dog racing, midget car racing, and even the county fair happened on the grounds of Playland Park. Redden promoted ball games, concerts, dances, contests, parades, pageants, and fireworks shows; nearly all of it best viewed from the old concrete grandstand in the apartment parking lot.

Those decrepit bleachers are built into a grassy ridge and are poorly protected by a roughshod chain-link fence. It's a façade that ought to evoke a sentimental mood but is spoiled by faded graffities and weeds that soar into the air like small trees; a reminder that whatever man does not destroy, nature will reclaim for her own. But for as long as they stand there, in defiance of every attempt to erase them, the bleachers will carry memories that soar far beyond the earliest years of American stock car racing.

That's because Tim Flock was not the only champion who claimed victory in front of these grandstands. This is also the place where the South Bend Blue Sox, inaugural and lifetime members of the All-American Girls' Professional Baseball League, completed the greatest season of their history, the summer before Flock took his checkered flag at the Playland Park Speedway. Baseball games had been played on the grounds as early as 1896, but it would be more than half a century before the place would ever see a championship.

Cheering fans filled the now-unkempt bleachers in July 1951 when South Bend Blue Sox pitcher Jean Faut threw a perfect game against the Rockford Peaches. When she struck out the last hitter to seal the perfecto, the crowd cheered, her teammates swarmed, and the South Bend Tribune proclaimed that:

Jean Faut, a sturdy gal with a lot of heart, a fast ball that hops, and a curve that breaks off like a country road, pitched a perfect no-hit, no-run game to subdue the Rockford Peaches, 2-0, at Playland Park Saturday night.

In 1953, Faut would hurl another perfect game, making her the only pitcher – male or female – to throw two such games in a career. But for all her success, Faut's career was not without drama. For starters, she was married to her team's manager, Karl Winsch, a man who got results but was not always popular with his players. This left Faut somewhere in the middle, and at other times left her nowhere at all. To the woman's credit, her performance on the field never suffered for the turmoil off of it.

Faut won an MVP in 1951, pitched that perfect game, and led the South Bend Blue Sox to the league championship in front of the hometown crowd at Playland Park. Faut was on the mound for the last seven innings of that final game, and when the last batter was retired, fans spilled from the bleachers to celebrate with the team on the field. Now it's only the bleachers that remain, barricaded like an exhibit at a museum, but in actuality the fence is not there to protect the bleachers from the people. It's there to protect the people from the bleachers, now designated an eyesore and a safety hazard.

These bleachers also bore witness to the 1952 Blue Sox season, one in which the whole world blew up and the team nearly disintegrated, but somehow ended with the hoisting of another trophy in South Bend. Jean Faut delivered her usual brilliance, but if there was anything else that could go wrong, it did. Tensions in the clubhouse had been brewing all season. Backups resented starters, young players resented veterans, and everyone resented Karl Winsch, including at one point, his own wife. For a few weeks, even Faut and Winsch were not on speaking terms.

At the end of August, with the season winding to a close and South Bend limping into a playoff spot, everything came to a head. Late in a game, with the result in hand, Winsch noticed one of his bench players prematurely changing out of her uniform. He called on her to pinch run for no reason than to embarrass her.

It worked.

There was a scene and a confrontation, there was a suspension and a mass walkout. When the dust cleared, the South Bend Blue Sox entered the playoffs with just twelve players left in the clubhouse, numbering a basketball squad instead of a baseball team. The 'Dutiful Dozen', as they became known, had their backs against the wall, but they also had Jean Faut. They advanced with ease into the best-of-five championship round before disaster struck again. The Blue Sox dropped two in a row to Rockford and found themselves on the brink of elimination.

Or maybe they didn't.

Winsch, in his boldest and grandest managerial move, protested the result of the second game on the grounds that the right field fence was too close to home plate. The league agreed with Winsch and voided the result of the second contest. When South Bend won the next matchup, the series was suddenly tied one game to one. After they'd won two more, the Blue Sox were once again the champions of the AAGPBL.

It's not a bad haul of history to be held within one parking lot, but then we're not done yet. After all, Jean Faut isn't even the greatest ballplayer to play the hero at this place. Maybe only the concrete bleachers, now sun-faded and rust stained, remember the time the greatest slugger in the history of the game came here to hit a baseball halfway to the river.

A quarter century before Tim Flock and Jean Faut, there was Babe Ruth.

It wasn't even two weeks after the dust had settled on the 1926 World Series that the advertisements appeared in publications all over South Bend. Babe Ruth and His Big League All Stars were coming to town for a two-game tilt against the South Bend Indians.

The games were to be played at Playland Park. Ticket prices were set at a dollar for adults and a quarter for children. The South Bend Tribune implored fans to spend the money and make the trip, because as the article warned, this was the last chance to see Babe Ruth in his prime since:

Ruth, like all other things and persons, is getting old.

7

This was just a pair of exhibition games, but Ruth's team wasn't quite the Harlem Globetrotters, and the South Bend squad was far from being the Washington Generals. In fact, the South Bend team featured a future Hall of Famer of its own in second basemen Freddie Lindstrom, as well as a future 200-game winner in Mishawaka native Freddie Fitzsimmons.

As for Ruth's team, they were mostly a handful of big-league also-rans and a smattering of players from lower-level east coast affiliated ball. The All Stars had a little more prestige than most of the rest of the South Bend team, but not much. Of course, the All Stars also had Babe Ruth at the peak of his powers, and that counts for something too.

The first game was played on Saturday, October 23 in front of a sold-out crowd. While Babe Ruth and His All Stars were taking the field at Playland Park, the Fighting Irish eleven were squeaking out a 6-0 victory at Northwestern, and a few of the louder ovations were reserved for the updates that were passed along the loudspeaker in between innings.

But the loudest ovations were saved for the Babe.

The South Bend nine actually held an early lead courtesy of an inside-the-park home run from center fielder Canary Napier, but Ruth's squad added runs in the fourth and fifth innings. By the time Ruth stepped to the plate with the bases empty in the sixth inning, his squad was already up 6-3.

It was about to be more.

Babe Ruth dug his spikes into a batter's box on a baseball diamond near the corner of Lincoln Way and Ironwood, and then, with night hastening and the game about to be called for darkness, the Sultan of Swat turned on a 1-2 offering from South Bend's Lefty Teague and blasted a rocket over the right field fence toward the St. Joseph River. The South Bend Tribune located the ball on the racetrack, some 605 feet from home plate. There's a young tree growing in a parking island at the place where the home run finally rolled to a stop.

Once he was around the bases, Ruth sought out a young fan, and gifted his bat – one that he'd used during the World Series! – to a six-year-old named Thomas Hoban.[1] After that, the umpire waved his arms and called the game on account of darkness. Babe Ruth and His All Stars had taken the first matchup by a score of 7-3.

If it's at all possible, Sunday's contest was even more hotly anticipated than the first one. For one thing, the South Bend team was trotting Freddie Fitzsimmons – a real big-league pitcher – out to the mound. But for all of the fanfare that accompanied South Bend's starter, there was even more excitement for the visiting

---

[1] I spent an entire week of my life trying to track down the whereabouts of this baseball bat. At long last, I was able to make contact with Tom Hoban's granddaughter in Cincinatti. She learned that the bat had been later given to Tom's cousin Maurice. I reached out to several of Maurice's children, many of whom are local to South Bend, but none recalled seeing the bat or ever being apprised of its existence.

hurler. That's because Babe Ruth, more than five years removed from his last big league pitching appearance, would be taking the pill for the All Stars.

There was just one problem. A cold front had come through overnight, accompanied by drizzle and sleet. It was an unpleasant day for baseball and only a few hundred fans showed up for the game. But to his credit, the Bambino made sure the game went on and that everyone in the crowd would get a show.

There were none of the fireworks of the previous day, but even without the home run, Babe Ruth was still a spectacle to behold. He lacerated a pair of singles and added a towering double over the course of four at-bats. On the mound, he scattered seven hits and allowed three runs. Fitzsimmons went pitch for pitch with the Babe, scattering seven hits of his own, and allowing the same number of runs. By the time the game was called on account of rain in the eighth inning, Canary Napier was wearing a topcoat in the outfield. The contest would go down in the box score as a weather-shortened 3-3 tie. That brought an end to the Bambino's tour of South Bend and brought the curtain down on the season for the Indians. The Tribune's coverage of the game concluded:

There will be no more baseball at Playland Park until the robins are twittering next spring.

On this day in August of 2022, as we begin our walk, we hear the twittering of the birds, but we do not see them, hidden as they are amongst the overgrowth and detritus that's become the bleachers where so many people watched so many things for so many years. We trace careful steps across sidewalks littered and bombed by armies of well-fed geese and somewhere out there we listen closely for the lost echoes of the sounds of Playland Park.

There are no sounds. There are no cheers from the crowd, there are no roars from the racecars, there are no nasally voices hawking peanuts, there is not the perfect crack of a wooden bat barreling a baseball, there is not the calliope of the steam-driven carousel, there are not the thundering footfalls of the raucous dance hall, there are not the dingings and ringings of the casino, there are not the exuberant splashes of children cannonballing into a massive swimming pool, there are not the whinnies of the horses as they are led to their gates, there is not the mechanical chunk-chunk-chunk of the old wooden roller coaster climbing to its peak, and there is not the whirring of the speeding coaster cars chased by the joyous screams of its riders on the way down.

There is only a muffled voice, communicating unintelligibly across an Arby's drive-through speaker at the place where the roller coaster used to be. For many years, that roller coaster was the crown jewel of Playland Park and in 1925, a local girl named Cecilia Lang won a prize of $25 in gold for bequeathing the coaster's new name:

The Jack Rabbit.

At a cost of $40,000, The Jack Rabbit was not a trifle of a fair ride, the kind set up by carnies in a matter of hours to thrill children who didn't know any better. It was a state-of-the-art, modern-for-its-time roller coaster that attracted visitors and thrill seekers from across the Midwest. Can you hear the rails a hummin'? From its highest heights, The Jack Rabbit offered a sweeping view of the park, the neighborhood, and the St. Joseph River; but the real highlights came with the screams and the thrills on the way back down again.

Of course, not everything is meant to last forever, and this is especially – but not exclusively – true of decades-old roller coasters. The AAGPBL went belly-up at the end of the 1954 season and took the Blue Sox down with them. NASCAR demanded faster cars and faster cars demanded longer tracks to race on. Thrill-seekers needed more than a nostalgic wooden roller coaster to satiate their ever-hungrier adrenaline rushes. The park was torn down and replaced with a nine-hole golf course as well as several commercial and retail buildings that have themselves been torn down in the decades since. Only the bleachers remain, watching quietly as everything else has been leveled and paved and leveled and paved all over again.

Flaubert feared sand. I fear parking lots.

And so, it comes about, as we continue on our walk, that we turn away from what used to be Playland Park to cross a red bridge over the wide river so that we can explore another place that used to be something else before it became a place to park cars.

The postcards and letterheads that boasted of the South Bend Watch Company painted the picture of a beautiful campus that housed production and business activities for several hundred employees; a red building with a stunning view of the St. Joseph

12

River, buttressed by a pair of idyllic, sputtering fountains, nestled comfortably beneath a perfect sky in a symphony of blue. That building isn't here anymore.

That building was never here.

It was a common trick of the time to hire artists to sketch an idealized version of a company's headquarters. It spelled success to would-be customers and sold a more perfect workplace to potential employees. As the South Bend Watch Company sought to entice experienced watchmakers from the eastern United States, their marketing materials became a key ingredient in the seduction. Hirings were conducted remotely, often by a weeks-long exchange of letters. By the time a new employee arrived in South Bend to survey his new workplace, there was no turning back. He'd already quit his job, sold his flat, and loaded up his possessions for a new life in Indiana. Gazing upon the parking garage that sits in the building's place today is as disappointing an experience as the old watchmaker might have felt when he looked upon his new workplace for the first time and noticed, in order, that: there were no fountains, the campus didn't actually have a view of the river, and the building wasn't even red.

Still, for what it lacked in promised beauty, the South Bend Watch Company made up for in pedigree, capital, and technology. Its earliest investors included Studebakers, Beigers, and Kamms; a veritable who's who of business royalty in St. Joseph County. The company was well-managed, well-funded, and opened to significant spectacle in March 1903. To hear the Daily News tell it:

President Studebaker Touches the Button that Sends an Electric Thrill through the Machinery of the Million Dollar Watch Factory

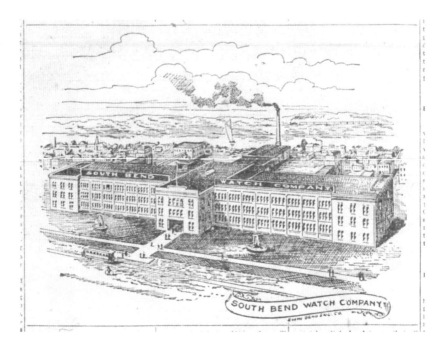

SOUTH BEND WATCH COMPANY

The company's earliest employees included more than 150 experienced watchmakers, all relocated to South Bend and armed with the most modern equipment of the day. The pocket watches they put out during the company's early history were considered fashionable, reliable, and competitive with similar watches coming out of New York and even Europe. When the Studebakers later lent their name and credibility to a line of railroad grade watches, the South Bend Watch Company looked like a runaway success. Then again, there had once been a day when it seemed like Playland Park would never close either.

In the aftermath of The Great War, the face of the world changed in big and profound ways that still reverberate throughout history. Maps were redrawn, geopolitical alliances were formed, governments were toppled and replaced, powers were shifted, and all of a sudden, men wanted to wear wristwatches.

That last one doesn't seem like a seismic shift in the same way those others do, but for the South Bend Watch Company it would prove to be the end of the world. In the early 1900s, wrist watches were considered effeminate. They were considered jewelry. Quality watchmakers rarely bothered with wristwatches because, to hear the misogyny of the day tell it, men didn't wear jewelry and women didn't need to tell time.

But when men enlisted in (or were drafted into) the service, they were assigned a utilitarian wristwatch as part of their standard set of gear. It didn't take long at all for soldiers to realize that wristwatches were actually quite useful and certainly less of a hassle than their pocket-borne kin. The stigma around the femininity of wristwatches evaporated when they became the preferred timepieces of *war-torn veterans*. In a startling instant, the pocket watch was a thing of the past.

The South Bend Watch Company didn't believe it would last. Their leaders maintained that wristwatches were a passing fad and decided not to make a wrist-worn version of their own timepieces. It wouldn't be long, they reasoned, before pocket watches reclaimed their rightful place in the American conscience, and when they did, the South Bend Watch Company would be positioned better than their more wistful competitors.

They were wrong.

When it proved that pocket watches would never return to fashion, it was too late for the South Bend Watch Company to pivot. They closed down operations at the end of 1929. The building burned down in 1957, the acreage rose again as a Coca-Cola bottler, and at long last, the land became a parking garage at the university, because of course it did; a flame that flickered one day and died away.

Time carries an eraser, but history carries a swift grey pencil, and what the eraser lacks in swiftness, it makes up for in dogged persistence. Maybe that's what makes it so surprising that Adams High School is still standing, nearly a century after it was opened two months late, and after several attempts to close it along the way. The school opened to delayed and muted fanfare in 1930, a casualty of a polio pandemic that swept through the area, a time that was later forgotten when angry people called the earliest parts of the Covid pandemic "unprecedented."

The great eraser made several attempts to wipe Adams High School off the map, and the building was discussed as a closure target in 1996 and 2001. By then, the 70-year-old building had fallen into disrepair, but the surrounding neighborhoods fought to save their school each time. Playland Park and the South Bend Watch Company may have been watching over the school when it was built from the ground up, but it's Adams that's stood long enough to watch all of those other places get torn down. Life goes on here, and even the grey skies are just clouds passing through.

Our walk continues along the sidewalks of River Park, once upon a time the county's first true suburbia. River Park was where you wanted to live, an upper-middle class paradise filled with people who looked with pride upon their homes and communities and knew that they'd arrived. But then I remember reading the faded microfilm about a different time, when this place was home to packs of feral dogs who would wander the night looking for something to kill. It's a microfilm that might belong to the most depressing issue in the long history of the South Bend Tribune. The paper begins with rampaging dogs ransacking the zoo, continues with the follies of the worst team in professional baseball, bloviates about the massively polluted water of Lake

Michigan, and in what passed as good news, shares the following dispatch from a Ku Klux Klan rally in nearby Osceola:

Fewer than Expected at White Pride Fest

The year was 2002, I had just graduated from high school, and by all appearances, the world was very much about to go to shit. We were all still reeling in the aftermath of 9/11, the Klan was coming back to set up camp in our own back yard, the Silver Hawks were struggling in standings and revenue so badly that a local bar invented a cocktail called the 40-100 (in dubious dishonor of the home team's record during a particularly miserable recent season), and yes, a pack of feral neighborhood dogs inexplicably broke into the Potawatomi Zoo to murder 14 wallabies and one black swan; injuring an ostrich, a kangaroo, and an additional wallaby along the way. I didn't feel bad about leaving South Bend to go to college, and I planned earnestly to never come back.

You'd be forgiven for believing that the only thing that moves faster than progress is destruction, but to do so would be to ignore the evidence of a cultural springtime that is evident in the River Park neighborhood today. Renewal follows decline follows renewal follows decline follows renewal follows decline and on the third day Christ was raised from the dead. Things get broken and fixed; even the prodigal son returns. We cross the Ironwood bridge as we continue our walk and the homeless man who sleeps in the tent along the narrow wood does not consider himself homeless because he knows his tent is his home. The only problem is the location, and when the box trucks jostle over the bridge in the wee hours of the morning to stock the shelves of what used to be the local grocer, they stir him from his peaceful slumber every single time. He'd like to move from the place he lives and there's nothing stopping him, but he stays there night after night for all the same reasons that I did for longer than I ever should have. Sometimes, home is only the place you become most accustomed to, and a remarkable trait of people is that they can become accustomed to awful things. The winsome eraser seems to leave those memories alone, and along the way, homes become foreign places and foreign places become homes.

At least that's what's happening here. A month after our walk, the lawns of the campus of the university will be filled with nearly 5,000 students from across the Midwest and across the world. The apartments on top of the old racetrack will become homes to many of them. Restaurants will be packed to capacity and the running trail will experience the thick traffic of ambitious young people trying to stay that way. Empty parking lots that sit in outright contumacy of the history that came before them will be filled with cars, and those cars will be filled with chattering people moving between stages in their lives, toting backpacks and building futures. They'll never get to ride The Jack Rabbit, but maybe someday, someone will look up at the decrepit concrete bleachers and wonder what those things are doing there.

And then, on the weekend, when it's time to let loose, they'll gather their liquor and their friends, fill their apartments beyond any comfortable capacity and they'll throw the greatest party they can imagine, but the bleachers will know better, because the bleachers will remember that the greatest parties in the history of South Bend happened right in front of them.

A proper day at Playland Park bled all the way into the night and sometimes into the next morning. August 8, 1936 was one of those proper days. Besides the usual trappings of the theme park and the swimming pool and the funhouse and the carousel and all of the other standard amusements, the track featured a performance from the daredevil and demolition derby group, The Death Dodgers. It was a lot, and it was all very loud, but it was just the beginning, because as the sun moved to set, the music started to play, and the party was set to begin.

Everything else had only been posturing and foreplay, a prelude to the kiss.

Duke Ellington was a star from the beginning, and his trajectory was always going to put him at Playland Park, one way or another. As a youngster growing up in Washington D.C., his first passion was baseball, and his first fan was none other than President Theodore Roosevelt. Ellington recalled that Roosevelt would often take a mid-afternoon break from his executive work to ride his horse around D.C. and that the Commander-in-Chief used to pause at their ball diamond to watch the boys play. Ellington would even rub shoulders with Washington's elite at

Senators games, where he was first employed as a peanut hawker during ballgames. Once he was a star, Ellington maintained his love for baseball, and would often stage impromptu games with his orchestra behind the tour bus. So if it hadn't been for music, perhaps it would have been baseball that delivered Ellington to South Bend.

But of course, there was the music, and Duke Ellington remains arguably the greatest jazz composer in the history of the genre. For everything that's been erased and forgotten, there may still be the echoes of Duke Ellington and His Famous Orchestra staged beneath a perfect Indiana summer night at Playland Park's own Melody Gardens. The paid advertisements ran for weeks in a South Bend Tribune that was loath to provide too much free publicity for a "colored" act. But when Duke Ellington came to town, there was no trouble getting the word out. The park was filled to capacity, and one has to wonder if there was ever any other place in the world where a person could ride a roller coaster, spectate a baseball game, swim in a pool, take in a demolition derby, and dance to the music of Duke Ellington, all with a single entry ticket and in a single day.

Anyway, that place doesn't exist anymore, but the bleachers still do, and despite the best efforts of the great rubber eraser, they're the only thing left.

CHAPTER TWO
THE BANDITTI OF THE PRAIRIES

The grist mill that stands over the entrance to Bonneyville Mill County Park in Bristol, Indiana is a throwback to a simpler time. Built in 1837, the structure is historically protected and remains the oldest continuously operated grist mill in the state of Indiana. Walking tours peruse its levels, offer views of its ancient wood and still-moving parts. Visitors can even purchase the flour that's still produced within the mill's walls.

According to the mill's own website, it is the most photographed and most painted spot within all of Elkhart County, and it's not hard to see why. Framed by a perfect forest and straddling the calm waters of the Little Elkhart River, the Bonneyville Mill is at once idyllic, pastoral, tranquil, and serene.

The man who put it there was none of those things.

Edward Bonney was an opportunist from New York who planted shallow roots wherever he went and who managed to live several lifetimes by the time he died in 1864 at the age of 56. He was at various times an entrepreneur, a criminal, a vigilante, a soldier, and a best-selling author. But before any of that, he was the founder of a brand-new town on the Indiana prairie.

Bonney platted the town of Bonneyville in 1837, dreaming of a town to call his own. Work began quickly on the grist mill that still stands, a sawmill that disappeared more than a century ago, and the Goshen Hotel.[2] All of it cost more money than Bonney had, but lenders were more than willing to step in. After all, the man owned his own town. What could go wrong? Even as his debts mounted, Bonney assured the banks that once the canal was

---

[2] Despite its name, the Goshen Hotel was very much in Bonneyville.

routed through Bonneyville, he'd be more than able to make good. The banks believed it and Bonney must have believed it too.

But the canal never came, and whether it was financial insolvency, impatience, or just the transient nature that would later define his life; Bonney abandoned his dream for the town in 1841. He sold off the hotel. He sold off the mills. He sold off the land. His time as a townbuilder had ended, but Edward Bonney was just getting started as an entrepreneur.

Bonney's second line of work was less honorable, but it appears to have been far more lucrative. It was less than a year after he left Bonneyville that the authorities began to suspect Bonney as a kingpin in a widespread counterfeiting network, one that had exploited certain loopholes in the young nation's laws. And while there was no doubt that what Bonney was doing was illegal, it was tough to nail down exactly how illegal it was or which entity was responsible for bringing a stop to it. After all, Bonney wasn't printing fake United States dollars.

He was counterfeiting pesos.

Used as tender in the south and along the furthest lines of western expansion, pesos spent just like official currency all over the frontier and even enjoyed a brief time as legal tender in the United States. It was a scheme that might have flown under the radar during a time when counterfeiting was rifer than it has ever been in the history of the west, but Bonney lacked nuance and restraint.

In order to attract the attention of the lawkeepers, he would need to be minting a lot of pesos, and it turns out that Bonney was minting an awful lot of pesos.

The man's career as a counterfeiter was even shorter than his career as a townbuilder. By 1842, Bonney was placed under arrest and sent to Indianapolis to await trial. If he were anyone else, his story might have ended there, but this was Edward Bonney. He was a cat as much as he was a man, and he still had seven lives to go.

Bonney escaped from his incarceration somewhere along the way to Indianapolis and fiddle-footed his way to Nauvoo, Illinois where his life was about to become much, much stranger. The details about how it all happened are unsatisfyingly deficient, but somehow, Edward Bonney ingratiated himself into the best graces of Joseph Smith, founder of the Mormon Church.

The creation of his new religion had not always been easy for Smith. Forced to abandon New York when whispers of punishment for his heresies turned into full blown threats, Smith relocated himself and his followers to Ohio. There, he was quite literally tarred and feathered by an angry mob, but it was bank fraud that finally forced his next move to Missouri. And when Smith endorsed the threats of a war that sought to "exterminate" all of the non-Mormon Missourians, he was imprisoned and his followers were forced out of that state as well. On the run and with their leader trapped behind bars to await trial, the Mormon faith hung on a string. They needed either a miracle or a scheme.

They got both.

Five years before Edward Bonney managed his own escape, Joseph Smith authored one of his own. After a grand jury hearing, Smith and a few cohorts escaped from custody and landed back amongst his followers in Nauvoo, where he introduced the doctrine of polygamy and began to build a literal army. Controversy followed the Mormons and their leader into Illinois and through Joseph Smith's failed presidential run in 1844. That's when Smith assembled a secret group called the Council of Fifty and gave the Council the authority to decide which state and federal laws Mormons were obligated to obey — and which ones they weren't. The Council was comprised of four dozen of the highest-ranking Mormons in the church as well as a certain Edward Bonney, who was famously not a Mormon.

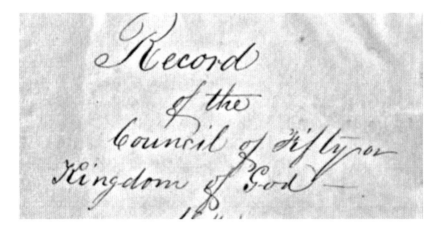

The former millwright, city planner, escaped counterfeiter, and itinerant fiddle-footer quickly became Joseph Smith's right-hand man, and besides his addition to The Council of Fifty, Bonney would be appointed as Smith's personal Secretary of War.

It was the shortest job he would ever hold.

Just five days after Bonney's appointment as *aide-de-camp*, Joseph and Hiram Smith were arrested and held for treason. Fearful that the Prophet would escape once again, a violent schism of dissenting Mormons descended upon the courthouse, intending to take care of the Smiths themselves.

Urged on by the Mormon dissenters, who were thirsting for blood, they collected, to the number of about one hundred and forty, armed and disguised, and proceeded to the jail... Having dispersed the guard they attacked the jail, and Joseph and Hiram Smith were both shot dead. Four balls pierced each of them, and any of the wounds would have proved fatal.

Smith's murder brought an end to Edward Bonney's brief stint as the most influential outsider in the history of the Church of Latter-Day Saints. For Bonney, that just meant it was time for another adventure.

There's something strangely admirable about Bonney's ability to admit when he was defeated and to move on to another of his eclectic interests and careers. Usually, it's the stubborn who are celebrated; brave men and women who stared down impossible odds and crawled back from defeat after defeat. Bonney was not one of those, but then, doesn't it take just as much bravado to recognize a bad situation, turn away from it –

even if it's all you've ever known – and build a brand-new life all over again?

Edward Bonney's next stop was in Iowa where he operated a livery by day and acted as a vigilante bounty hunter by night. By all accounts, his work was welcomed, sanctioned, and appreciated by local law enforcement. There was plenty of work to be done, outwitting organized groups of bandits who were ransacking and looting their way across the burgeoning western frontier. It was bad for the pioneers, but it was good for Bonney's burgeoning business. In fact, it was about to make him famous.

The torture-murder of Colonel George Davenport was the kind of macabre story that delivered attention and disgust toward the outlaws of the wild west. Davenport was a hero of some acclaim in his community; in fact, Davenport, Iowa is named in his honor. So when he was murdered by a gang of hoodlums on the Fourth of July, the story filled the front pages and an entire nation clamored for justice.

But tracking down and bringing an end to the *Banditti of the Prairie* was not going to be easy. It was going to require guile and resolve, and given the eclectic nature of Edward Bonney's life, it's possible that there was not another man in the world with the requisite experience to crack the case. In order to track down the four men responsible, Edward Bonney would need to call on every bit of his radically varied experience.

His brief time in Nauvoo had exposed him to pockets of criminals who hid among the Mormon communities where they would claim to be persecuted saints whenever officers of the law stepped into the town's theocratic limits. Bonney recognized the hallmarks of those criminals in the Davenport case, but suspicion wasn't proof, and so Edward Bonney went undercover in the gang's ranks, posing convincingly as a counterfeiter. No one seemed to wonder why the ruse came so naturally to him.

Bonney interrogated dozens of people across the Midwest, dodging angry Mormons and vindictive bandits along the way. Then, once he was armed with the dossier of evidence he needed to make his case, Bonney chased a quartet of killers across all of his old stomping grounds – Illinois, Missouri, Indiana, and Ohio – before finally bringing them to justice and to the hangman.

But the story didn't nearly end there, at least not for Edward Bonney. His actions may have been noble and heroic, but they placed him squarely on the wrong side of a bloodthirsty gang that operated across parts of four different states. Bonney would spend the rest of his days dodging threats against his life.

I was told... I should have my throat cut and
my body chopped into mince-meat.

Given the nature of those threats, it might have been prudent for Bonney to avoid notoriety and infamy, at least for a while. It might have been a good idea to lay low for a while, except that he didn't know how to. For his next act, instead of eschewing the spotlight, he invited it. He recalled and recorded everything he knew about the Banditti.

And then he wrote a book about it.

The Banditti of the Prairies was an early hit and an immediate bestseller. It was a true crime piece before true crime was a genre. The book is not well-written, but the story it tells is satisfyingly salacious. What's more, when compared against the court records, it appears to be a fairly accurate retelling of the events he describes. His writing style is ridiculously verbose. Upon further review, many long paragraphs turn out to be out-of-control run-on sentences. Even the full title of tome spans three dozen words:

The Banditti of the Prairies, or the Murderer's Doom
A Tale of Mississippi Valley and the Far West
An Authentic Narrative of Thrilling and Hair Breath
Adventures in the Early Settlement of the Western Country

In many ways, Edward Bonney was a man of his time. In others, he was far ahead of it. Through a tangled web of observably convoluted pages, Bonney manages to deliver his readers directly into the seediest hideouts of the most ruthless criminals. The intrigue of his narrative does not come from the view through the lens of the detective, but instead from the voyeuristic gaze he directs toward dens of depraved killers and thieves. The book has less in common with campy noir spy novels than it does the proliferation of modern documentaries and podcasts that take viewers into the lives and minds of the most notorious serial killers. In at least this way, and in many more, Bonney was a trailblazer. His promise to his readers panders unashamedly toward their more sadistic natures as Bonney promises from the very beginning of his story:

Before entering fully upon our tale of blood, which will thrill every heart with a shuddering sense of the brutality of man...

Every literate adult felt the pull to explore the underworld that The Banditti of the Prairies promised to deliver even if they were loath to admit it. Edward Bonney, against all odds, had turned himself into a star and a prominent national figure.

Of course, none of that was enough to prevent him, just a year later, from sitting in a court room during a shady trial where he was credibly accused of murder. But this was not the end of the man's story either. It might have cost another of his nine lives, but Bonney was fully acquitted of the charges. He moved to Chicago where he became the postmaster at Prospect Park and lived a quieter life for the better part of a decade.

But Edward Bonney wasn't built for a quiet life, and as it turns out, he wasn't built for a quiet death either. In 1862, at the ripe age of 56, Edward Bonney enlisted into the Union Army to fight in the Civil War. His time in the more formal military was brief, just like his time almost everywhere had been brief. Bonney took a bullet to the leg at the Siege of Vicksburg and died because of that wound a few months later. When he was paralyzed and confined to a hospital bed aware that his luck had run out and his moment was approaching, Bonney might have identified with the villains from his story as they awaited the gallows:

Hopelessly, entirely now, the prisoners were forced to submit to their certain fate, and passing the hours within the lonely confines of their prison cells, watched the sunbeams as they crept upon the dusty walls, and counted the moments as they passed, hastening them toward the day of their execution.

In February of 1864, Edward Bonney returned to Bonneyville for the first time since he sold the place; this time in a box and buried with military honors at the Bonneyville Cemetery. His town may not have been a success, but his book has never left print, and of course, his mill is still producing, a quiet and serene relic that has almost nothing in common with the man who built it.

CHAPTER THREE
A VOICELESS CHORUS CHANTING
THAT THE OLD TIMES WERE BEST

The mourners file somberly from the weathered brick building, the arched glass doorway the only piece of the fading structure that feels refreshed. Women dab their eyes and turn back into the fray for last hugs, spotting old friends that haven't been in this building for quite some time. Children, now grown, pause at an old Sunday school classroom, their sadnesses measured and calculated; then deemed an appropriate portion of lament by the reserved nods of their grandparents. A couple clings tightly to one another as they descend the front steps. Although they have attended this church every Sunday for a half-a-century, it's been years since they've passed through the front doors and down these steps; but then it seems undignified to be sneaked down the ramp and out the back on a day such as this one. They remember the time they passed down these steps so many years ago, her in a dress and him in a suit, their friends showering them with a confetto of dry rice, his father's boss's fine car parked on the street, all theirs for just that one weekend. This funeral has proved a homecoming for those who have left the Church or for those who have left this church, and the place was filled with just as much energy the day before when the rememberers descended on the building to clean and polish the pews; to make immaculate the grounds; to attempt to lift carpeted Communion stains that had outlasted the past three tenures of the past three pastors. Had an Easter in this building ever seen a grandeur like this? The people reminisce about the golden olden glory of the days gone by, always remembering things a little better than they actually were. On this day, the old place sparkles and it is a shame that for so many of us, the finest suit we will ever wear will be dressed upon us at our own funerals. There is no casket, there is no urn, and there is no hearse. There are eulogies, but there is no obituary. After not quite a century, the church has closed up and its congregation has been dissolved. It takes a long time for the sauntering parade to end, but when it does, the last man out locks the doors behind them and then stares a long time at the key, not knowing what to do with it anymore.

It's a scene that will be repeated without much variance at more than 100 churches across the United States on this day, congregations that are struggling and failing, consolidating and moving, dying and leaving, remembering reverent revelry without ever facing forgotten failures that foment a faithful finality. The mourners will find themselves around tables dressed with cloths in tiny kitchens, itchy and warm in Sunday's best, and they will wonder to themselves if it all could have been different. For thirty years, the carpenter and the schoolteacher who lived in the white house around the block had faithfully paid their tithe every week on every Sunday and their building had closed anyway. Even a banker could never be so callous and at least a mortgage has terms.

Whatever happened to the shepherd who would leave the ninety-nine for the one? Anyway, someone – or someones – has made a decision that will remove them from their Family and their Home all in a single day, and it doesn't matter if it was the right decision or the only decision or the inevitable decision:

It will never stop hurting.

There are deep holes that no amount of pavement can fill.

The single father remembers that this had been the only family he had in the months after his divorce, and now he's been removed from that family too.

The man who used to be the church's janitor recalls praying in the pews of the sanctuary in the midst of his deepest depression and his most vivid thoughts of suicide, and when all of those thoughts begin to return, the place is closed to him and there is nowhere else to go.

*   *   *

The old church at the corner of Ewing and High Streets opened its doors for the first time in July 1916, and by all rights, the dedication of a new sanctuary should have been front page news in South Bend, Indiana. The free publicity might have been a boon for membership and might have set off a ripple effect that would have ended with something other than the closing of the church in the Year of Our Lord 2022.

But it had been a busy summer and a chaotic weekend in Indiana and across the world. For months, the front page had been dominated with headlines from a European war that was threatening to pull the United States into its orbit. The day before the little church opened, the newspapermen carried alarming dispatches from a terrorist attack in San Francisco. Leftists had bombed a Preparedness Parade, killing ten and injuring forty more. All of it would have unsettled the excited pastor of the new congregation in South Bend, who for months had planned and plotted the grand sermon to mark the occasion of his church's christening, only to watch it all unravel in the hours before the ceremony. His grand message would have to wait. For now he would have to respond to the news of the day and reassure his flock amidst the ever-growing whispers of war and shouts of violence.

But that wasn't all. The announcement of the little church's parturition was pushed even off of the second and third pages of the South Bend Tribune that day, all in honor of the mourning tears that spilled across the state and the country when the bulletins shared that James Whitcomb Riley, The Hoosier Poet, had died.

For a generation of Americans at the turn of the century, Riley was an enormous public figure – a prevalent voice in their lives, the leading poet of his day, and among the most commercially successful writers of his time. Even President Woodrow Wilson was left grieving at the news of Riley's demise:

May I not express to you my sincere sorrow at the death of James Whitcomb Riley? With his departure a notable figure passes out of the nation's life; a man who imparted joyful pleasure and a thoughtful view of many things that other men would have missed. I am sure I am speaking the feeling of the whole country in expressing my feeling of loss.

The handful of people who knew Riley during his brief time in St. Joseph County would have been shocked that the poet became a man whose passing garnered a statement from the President, let alone that flags would be flown at half-mast or that he would be featured on a postage stamp. It was just for a few months in 1873 that Riley worked as a sign-painter for Stockford & Blowney in South Bend, but he was drunk for most of it and incurred so much debt at South Bend restaurants and saloons that it would take him eight years to get it all paid off.

Somehow or another, the drunken signmaker transformed himself into one of his country's leading voices, its most successful poet, and his home state's biggest celebrity. By the 1890s, Riley was a bestselling author and toured the country performing readings of his greatest hits. He was celebrated nationwide with an annual Riley Day while he was still very much alive and is considered the father of what's known as The Golden Age of Indiana Literature. When he returned to South Bend for a performance in 1900, he was given a hero's welcome and the newspapers hailed him as a born genius, even waxing about his abilities as painter:

...one of Riley's hand-painted picket fences was a rapture to even the most exacting eye.

It seemed for a while that Riley could do no wrong. He befriended business magnates and politicians, amassed a fortune, and was even bandied as a candidate to become America's first Poet Laureate. He sold millions of copies of his books and enjoyed fame and notoriety wherever he went. The highs of his life had been very high, but then James Whitcomb Riley died, and before he could even be laid to rest, his legacy would be torn down and paved over the same way as anything else.

Critics were quick to seize on the inauthenticity of Riley's Hoosier dialect poems. Although he found his greatest success as a humble, rural poet; Riley had been raised as the son of a lawyer and lived much of his life in cities. The dialect he employs to achieve his trademark folksy affect often feels infantilized and imagined. More scathing critics complained that he set back the advancement of a burgeoning American literature scene with his use of hillbilly English in turns of phrases like these:

> *You better not fool with a Bumblebee!—*
> *Ef you don't think they can sting—you'll see!*
> *They're lazy to look at, an' kind o' go*
> *Buzzin' an' bummin' aroun' so slow,*
> *An' ac' so slouchy an' all fagged out,*
> *Danglin' their legs as they drone about*

In 1877, Riley submitted one of his own works to newspapers claiming that it was one of the lost poems of Edgar Allen Poe, but the ruse was found out when newspapers disbelieved the hoax on account of the poem being so bad that it was impossible Poe could have ever written it. In the years before his death, Riley's friends begged him to stop composing new works, afraid their poor quality would damage his legacy. He would not heed their advice, and literary history has come to regard Riley as unserious and untalented, a middling children's poet who should have never dabbled beyond an elementary school reading level.

The Indiana Bard began his career thanks to an endorsement from Henry Wadsworth Longfellow and would become Longfellow's antecedent in every meaningful way after that. He was wildly successful in life, dismissed and forgotten in death, then expunged from the western canon altogether. If he were aware of his post-mortem fall from grace, then perhaps he could take solace in the words of one of his famous poems, "A Life-Lesson":

There! little girl; don't cry!
They have broken your doll, I know;
And your tea-set blue,
And your play-house, too,
Are things of the long ago;
But childish troubles will soon pass by. –
There! little girl; don't cry!

It's a strange sentiment for a children's poem and a broken sentiment for adults. The awareness of the inevitability of loss has never shielded anyone from feeling its stinging pain. The destruction of a man's life has never stung any less knowing that someday and somehow, it would have all been destroyed anyway. Modern critics treat analysis of Riley's poetry as fruitless, as if his work is somehow below criticism. It's hard to imagine Riley himself would be comforted by the fact that years after his poetry was ridiculed and mocked, it would be largely forgotten. If Riley's sentiment is true, then that means that the words on a tomb are nothing more than haphazard markings on a rock and a grave is nothing but an empty hole waiting to be filled. The Indiana bard ought to have known better, if not in life, then certainly in death, because few corpses have learned the importance of a proper burial more than James Whitcomb Riley's.

The poet died without a will, without a spouse, and without children. With no one to carry out his last wishes, his body was stored for some fifteen months while a pair of Indiana cities played tug-of-war with the remains. Greenfield laid the first claim for the bard's bones; reasoning that he should be buried at the place he was born, with his father, mother, sister, and brother at his side. The Indianapolis Star even ran the headline a few days after Riley's death:

Burial to be at Greenfield

It wasn't quite that simple. Indianapolis also laid claim to Riley's body, and negotiations between the two cities were ongoing, often stalled, and always contentious. Indianapolis had been Riley's home for the last twenty-five years of his life and they wanted him badly. It would have been a good get for the young city to hold such a famous and noteworthy skeleton. Politics were played and money was raised and a monument was built and more than a year after his death, James Whitcomb Riley was at last buried in Crown Hill Cemetery at the highest point in Indianapolis, displacing a set of unknown and unmarked bones that had been there first.

In South Bend, where Riley had made himself into an indebted alcoholic, the Riley moniker is most famous for being the name of city's second high school[3], constructed and opened in 1924, then torn down and built all over again in 2000. The signs that he painted for Stockford & Blowney are faded and destroyed and the company that paid him to make them is lost to history. His poems are not a part of any standard curriculum in South Bend's schools. But say this for James Whitcomb Riley: The view from his grave in Indianapolis is the best in that entire city and his monument is visited often, even if it's by adventure seekers and landscape photographers instead of mourners.

---

[3] Riley High School's most famous alum is probably congresswoman Jackie Walorski, who was killed in an automobile accident a few weeks before I wrote these paragraphs. Mark Waters, most famous as the director of the Lindsay Lohan movie 'Mean Girls', is also a Riley graduate.

In the space of land between the shuttered church and the departed poet's educational namesake, there's something else that's just as old as both of them, and in order to see it, for the first time in a decade, I'm going golfing. The Studebaker Course on Ewing Street was once the grandest course in the city (because it started off as the only course in city[4]), but them days is past and gone and old Time's tuck his toll. Today, it's primarily used by youngsters learning the game and hackers who have no idea what they're doing. In other words, it's perfect for me.

Armed with a set of borrowed clubs that are arguably too short for my lanky frame, I'm set to enjoy one of the remaining traces of the Studebaker legacy. This place was originally a park, was conscripted as farmland during World War 1, then gifted to the city and transformed into a municipal golf course at the behest of Clem Studebaker. The land didn't provide enough acreage for a full-length course, but nine holes were better than nothing, and as far as my game is concerned, I've got a much better chance of breaking a hundred here than on a complete eighteen. I'm also excited by a newspaper review of the links from way back in 1921:

Under the direction of the park commissioners during the past few years Studebaker Park has been made one of the beauty spots of fairy charm and the new nine hole golf course which lies off of Calvert st. is said to be one of the finest municipal golf courses in the country.

---

[4] Studebaker proudly lays claim to being the first course in South Bend, a statement that is technically true, but might be a little disingenuous. The South Bend Country Club opened five years before Studebaker but exists outside of the city limits.

If the Studebaker Course has a signature element, it's the century-old trees that soar high above the fairways. I found many of those trees with my drives and I recognize that the place would have played easier a hundred years ago, or at least that's my excuse. But I'm happy to have kept the ball within the fences without destroying a window or braining a pedestrian. Houses line the east side of the course, their walls running right up against the barriers. North and south and west find the morning sounds of the neighborhood, cars on commute, students walking to school, dogs sniffing for just the right spot to mark their morning stroll. It's a nice enough place to spend a morning, but there's always some claustrophobia with an urban course and it's not different here.

A century ago, advertisements for these neighborhoods filled the local newspapers. It was the new best place to live in South Bend, what with its new golf course and new high school and new church and new homes. In the years since, the high school is the only thing that's been demolished and replaced. A century later, everything else on the surrounding blocks has turned 100-years-old. There's a charm to a part of the city that remains so reminiscent of the way it was built, but then of course, charm wasn't ever going to be enough to save the neighborhood church.

There! little girl; don't cry!
They have broken your slate, I know;
And the glad, wild ways
Of your schoolgirl days
Are things of the long ago;
But life and love will soon come by. -
There! little girl; don't cry!

43

It's not too far from here that Studebaker successor and corporate saboteur Albert Erskine built a course of his own, an 18-hole layout constructed with money he didn't have in order to satisfy the demands of a reputation he hadn't earned. Opened in 1925, the course was not the first of Erskine's ego-feeding actions and it would not be the last.

It was 1918 when Erskine published his History of the Studebaker Corporation, a work that drastically overstates his own contributions to the company. More than half of its pages are dedicated to the happenings during Erskine's three years as President of the then sixty-year-old company.

It was 1919 when Erskine began construction on his own stately mansion, a place originally called Twyckenham Park before the man decided that his home should be named after himself. It was a trend that would continue for quite some time. Erskine Manor remains, even today, situated upon Erskine Manor Hill Drive; the kind of home that demanded the printing of its own postcards:

Twyckenham Park, South Bend, Ind.

Home of A. R. Erskine, President of Studebaker Corp.

The trouble with Erskine's extravagance was that although he was well-compensated as Studebaker's president, he was not its owner. He was rich, but not fabulously so. For Albert Erskine, the truth of his bank account was of no matter and the appearance of wealth was always more important than the possession of it. This was a man who financed his image on mountains of debt, a charlatan a hundred years ahead of his time, and you'd be correct if you assumed Erskine also kept a winter estate in Florida. If he couldn't play on the same field as the big boys, maybe he could pretend like he did, and Erskine was nothing if not a skilled pretender. He was always willing to inflate, exaggerate, and bend truths in order to sell himself as the man he wanted others to believe he was, and it wasn't just his own life that Erskine was willing to hyperbolize about. It was the success of his company too.

It was August 1922 when the South Bend News-Times reported on Erskine's gaudy, disingenuous, and deliberately misleading announcement:

Studebaker Now Second Only to Ford in Motor Industry

The South Bend News-Times called the presentation a "romance in figures and in remarkable growth." For Albert Erskine, it might well have been a fiction.

Technically speaking, Erskine wasn't telling an outright lie. Studebaker was second to Ford in cash assets. It was second to Ford in the cost and size of its plants. It was second to Ford in the "value of its sales," a nuanced term that does not mean the same thing as net sales.

In the most important metrics – revenue, profits, market share, and cars on the road – Studebaker was doing well, but not quite as well as Erskine wanted the world to believe. Erskine's announcement should have been lauded as a harbinger for future growth but was treated instead as the moment when Studebaker had ascended to the top of some corporate mountain.

Trouble was, there was still a lot of climbing to go.

It's a small bit of poetry and something more than irony that one only needed to turn to the second page of the August 1 issue of the 1922 South Bend News-Times before being confronted by another headline and another news story. It turns out The Studebaker Corporation had a problem that required top-of-the-line professional help. An apocalyptic rat infestation had taken over their factory. Somewhere beneath the shiny veneer of Erskine's triumphant proclamation and on the next page of the local newspaper, there was evidence that things weren't as good as they seemed.

But that wasn't going to stop Albert Erskine.

While Ford and its competitors were doubling down on consolidating their market shares and investing in research and development, Erskine popped the corks on the champagne. He announced an increase on the annual dividend that would be paid to stockholders, as well as a special one-time bonus dividend to be paid out the next month. After all, the announcement's purpose wasn't to share a corporate truth; it was to further endear Albert Erskine to men who were wealthier than he was. 1922 was the beginning of a trend, and for the better part of the next decade, Erskine would work harder to guarantee the esteem of his stockholders than the success of his company.

The most important truth in Erskine's 1922 statement was about Studebaker's cash assets. At the beginning of the 1920s, Studebaker did hold more cash than any car company not named Ford. Those assets should have provided the great war chest they used to lay a foundation for the next 100 years of automotive greatness. Instead, Erskine raided those savings accounts immediately as part of a self-satisfying fiscal bacchanalia that would eventually spell the company's downfall.

Erskine's ego was an appetite that couldn't be satiated. He named the golf course after himself in 1925 and named a car after himself in 1927. For a time, Albert Erskine even managed to sponsor and name college football's championship trophy after himself. It was a sponsorship financed by debt and deception and would be awarded twice to Notre Dame during its first two seasons before being snatched away by USC in 1931. But by then, Erskine's ego had incurred a debt it wouldn't be able to keep. The car that bore his name was discontinued by 1931. The championship trophy was discontinued in 1932. His company declared bankruptcy in 1933, and he was removed from Studebaker's presidency at the same time.

By the summer of 1933, Erskine's house of cards had begun to crumble. He was unemployed and deeply in debt. Plenty of men who built their lives on more solid foundations than this had seen their legacies disintegrate far more quickly than Albert Erskine. But when faced with the inevitability of it all, on July 1, 1933; Erskine stepped into the bathroom of Erskine Manor[5] and turned his revolver upon himself, a suicide note at his side, stating simply:

I Cannot Go On

---

[5] It is oft reported that Erskine killed himself in the clubhouse at the Studebaker Proving Grounds near what is now Bendix Woods. This is an urban legend. The newspapers, Erskine's family, and his death certificate show that the suicide occurred at his home.

The morning's newspapers were flush with praise for the man's life, his contributions to Studebaker, and laments that the city had lost a great benefactor. It would be months and years and decades before people began to learn that his life and his contributions and his benevolence were a vapor and a fraud.

Still, Albert Erskine's name adorns a road and a shopping center and a neighborhood and a golf course. His old mansion is still there and my friend Mike the Librarian, had the privilege of informing the newest owner that Mr. Erskine had offed himself in her master bathroom.

The foolish man built his house on the sand; the rains came down, the streams rose, the winds blew and beat against that house, and against all odds, in the middle of a city wrecked by his own arrogance, Albert Erskine's legacy remains intact even as the worst parts of his life have largely been forgotten.

There! little girl; don't cry!
They have broken your heart I know;
And the rainbow gleams
Of your youthful dreams
Are things of the long ago;
But Heaven holds all for which you sigh. -
There! little girl; don't cry!

CHAPTER FOUR

THE FIRST SHOT OF THE GREAT WAR

The United States had done everything they could to avoid the war. Isolationists pointed out that the assassination of Franz Ferdinand had nothing to do with Americans. It was a European war, after all – an expensive, dangerous, and deadly conflict on the other side of the ocean. The story of America began when people left Europe behind for good. There was no sense in going back.

For his part, Woodrow Wilson seemed to agree with the pacifists and the isolationists. He did not want to be a part of the war either. But as the tides of conflict turned and as jingoistic newspapermen riled up the hawks, German U-boats began sinking vessels indiscriminately, threatening American lives and business interests. War was coming to the United States, and it would come with or without America's consent.

By April 1917, already three years into the conflict, Wilson didn't have a choice. The war had fallen into stalemate and the world was burning around him. He needed to be assured of a favorable outcome for America's interests and allies. Wilson asked Congress for "a war to end all wars" and Congress obliged him.

If war was a difficult thing for European nations to prepare for, it was a nightmare for the Americans. Moving young men from one corner of the country into a hasty boot camp arranged in another was a logistical difficulty. Getting nearly five million troops to the other side of the planet seemed an impossibility. An April declaration of war was no silver bullet to end the conflict. In fact, it would be nearly half-a-year before American troops were contributing to combat in significant ways.

Preparedness bills had been passed in the months prior, but American forces were still far from being ready to be mobilized. Boot camps were arranged, volunteer soldiers were solicited, and six weeks after the declaration of war, Congress gave Wilson the power to institute a draft. Men aged 21-45 were required to register for military service, including those who would later go on to make a splash at Playland Park in South Bend. Babe Ruth and Duke Ellington were both among those who filled out registration cards.

Back in South Bend, in the weeks before men were compelled to register in the draft, volunteer soldiers and combat veterans who'd served in the Spanish-American War were saying goodbye to their families, ironing out their old uniforms, and reporting for duty in service to their country.

Alexander Arch was one of those men. Arch had bounced back and forth between jobs at Oliver and Singer after the conclusion of the Spanish-American War, where he spent time stationed at the Mexican border during Pershing's campaign against Pancho Villa. For Arch, a declaration of war was a chance to advance his military career and to defend the freedom – however imperfect – his family had found in the United States.

Born in what was then Austria-Hungary and what is now Romania, Arch arrived in South Bend with his family in 1903. Arch was seven years old when his parents decided it was time to forge a fresh start in America. Although the Arch family managed to scrape together a living, the land of opportunity didn't immediately deliver on its enormous promise; at least not for the Arches and for dozens of Hungarian families like his own.

*   *   *

The first Hungarians to arrive in South Bend didn't fully know what they'd gotten themselves into. John Kovács led a ragtag group into town, lured by a promise he'd heard whispered across Europe. The only problem was that neither Kovács nor his companions spoke a lick of English, and as the first Hungarians in the city, that meant that no one spoke any of their language either.

After a few difficult days, Kovács was able to summon the tiny bit of German he knew in order to communicate with a friendly shopkeeper. The shopkeeper agreed to serve as an intermediary – Kovács translating his Hungarian thoughts into German and the shopkeeper translating the German words into English ones. The crew found lodging and unglamorous employment, but they were not above the difficult work, convinced that better opportunities would come their way.

Opportunities came slower than Kovács and his compatriots would have liked. Companies were slow to embrace

Hungarians, often viewing them as too transitory to employ in permanent roles. It was the kind of xenophobia that accompanied every major wave of European immigration to the United States, one that was difficult to overcome without the patronage of an important and established individual. Father Sorin had stepped up to vouch for the Irish. The Olivers had been willing to provide opportunity to the Poles. The Hungarians were left to wait for someone to notice their mettle and take up their cause.

As a consequence of the *gypsy* stereotype and provable work ethic that accompanied the earliest Hungarians, they were often given the hardest, dirtiest, and most dangerous jobs available. Promotions were rare. Injuries were common. Some two decades into their arrival, they'd failed to gain the esteem that had been given to other groups of European immigrants, and so the South Bend Hungarians doubled down on their efforts to care for themselves, establishing sick benefit societies, churches, social clubs, and even its own section of the city, dubbed Little Budapest. When Our Lady of Hungary parish was established in 1916, it marked a high point in the legitimacy of the Hungarian community, at least in its own eyes. Hungarians even had a local newspaper in their own language. The Városi Élet (translated "City Life") was in print in South Bend all the way through 1956.

And yet, despite their many successes, there were still hurdles for the Magyar to climb. When Kovács and his brother were naturalized as American citizens, they were sent to different courtrooms to swear their oaths in front of different judges. When their citizenship rites were completed, each judge Americanized each man's last name in different ways. To this day, South Bend is home to Kovaches and Kovatches who comprise one large family despite the variant spellings of their last names.

If they felt disrespected at all when they were separated from their family's name, those earliest Hungarians didn't show it. Instead, they did what they always did. They showed up for work and did whatever was asked of them. Eventually, the Hungarians would earn not just the respect of their city, but the admiration and celebration of the community that surrounded them. It was just going to have to come from an unexpected place.

*   *   *

General John Pershing was a man who was ready to go. While hundreds of thousands of soldiers across the United States kissed their mothers goodbye and loaded into train cars destined for bootcamps across the country, Pershing was already mobilizing his men for the European conflict. He recalled many of the platoons and soldiers who served with him during the Spanish-American War, and by July, his American Expedition Forces arrived in France to train alongside the European armies, months ahead of the newly conscripted soldiers who would follow behind.

Pershing was not a patient man, and indeed, most generals aren't. By October, he was pushing toward the Western Front, driving artillery units toward the village of Bathelemont in north France. Battery C was the first group to arrive in range and the first to maneuver their guns into position. Shortly after 6:00 in the morning on October 23, Battery C called to fire, and a French-manufactured 75mm explosive round was sent through the sky toward a German artillery battery. Whether the shot connected with its target didn't matter. The announcement was enough. The Americans were officially in the war.

The man who made the announcement stood at the other end of the gun, one hand still on the lanyard that launched the round into the early morning mist. The brave South Bender and native Hungarian, Sergeant Alexander Arch, had just fired the first American shot of the Great War.

The shot made Arch a national hero and the subject of profile pieces in the Washington Times and the New York Times. At the war's end, Arch received a three-minute standing ovation when he appeared before the House of Representatives. He marched in victory parades across the nation. During the coming years, Arch would be selected as a mourner during the burial of the Unknown Soldier and would even meet President Harding in D.C. The government would capitalize on Arch's name and face again during the lead-up to World War 2, trotting him out to sell war bonds. Arch made front page news all over again when he reenlisted to help fight the Nazis. Although he was not conscripted and never saw action, Arch's endorsement was service enough.

Alexander Arch even rubbed shoulders with Hollywood starlets and was among the last people to see actress Carol Lombard[6] alive. She died in a tragic plane crash just hours after appearing alongside Arch at a 1941 Indiana war rally.

With a single shot, Arch had become a celebrity. He'd become a symbolic hero for the entire nation. And for the Hungarian families in the neighborhoods back in South Bend, he'd become the legitimizing figure they'd been waiting for.

The mayor designated October 29, 1919 as Alex Arch Day in the city and the county commissioners approved a $2,000 expenditure to help plan the festivities. Even Albert Erskine got in on the welcome wagon, gifting Arch a car and offering him a plum job with Studebaker, which Arch accepted. Despite his insistence that he had no plans to marry, because "one war was enough," Arch did eventually settle down with a South Bend girl named Julia, and the pair would raise four children together.

---

[6] Ranked by AFI as one of the top 25 actresses of classic Hollywood, Lombard was born and raised in Fort Wayne, Indiana. Despite her acclaim and many successful roles, she is arguable most famous for being married to Clark Gable.

What was good for Arch was also good for his Hungarian friends and neighbors. The stereotype of the Magyar was that they were too transient and gypsylike. There was a persistent question about whether or not they were *true Americans*. But when one of their own became America's war hero, there wasn't much room for xenophobia anymore. After all, maybe only Steve Rogers and Uncle Sam were more perfectly American than Alexander Arch:

Look at his face for a minute and see why the American forces were the decisive factor in winning the war.

High cheek bones, deep-set eyes, sharp nose, narrow at the base, head high from the ears up, with plenty of room for brains; firm mouth, square, determined jaw; straight shoulders.

No coward, no poltroon ever had a face like that. It belongs to the kind of men who may be slow to fight but are equally slow to stop until victory is won.

Sergeant Arch's own story shows that he is a "before breakfast" fighter. Here is what he says of that first shot:

"The French major came over to where we were and told Captain I. R. McLendon to begin firing. Then the captain gave the order, and we fired the first shot at five minutes and ten seconds after 6 o'clock on the morning of October 23, 1917. We hit a bridge at Strassburg, in Alsace-Lorraine, German territory, and blew up the German working party there—a regular bull's-eye. After that we fired seventeen more shots, which took about two hours. Then we went to breakfast."

There are a good many victories won before breakfast.

But they are not with the eyes shut or the head on a pillow.

You have to be up and doing EARLY to be first in almost anything.

Hundreds of great victories—mental and physical, commercial, scientific, victories of every kind—are won in that first splendid hour after a good night's sleep. Don't waste that hour.

In the years that followed, Hungarians began to see the raises and promotions that had eluded them during their first years in the city. Second-wave immigrants found the education and skills they needed to work as professionals, not just as laborers.

And despite their success as Americans, the Hungarians – more than almost any other cohort in South Bend – maintained their roots. They erected Hungarian bakeries and restaurants and clubs. Julius Fodor built the Indiana Theater just a few blocks from Arch's home. The theater would show Hungarian-language plays and films, including a performance by Hungarian film star, Pál Jávor.

It hadn't been easy, but the South Bend Hungarians had become fully appreciated within their city without compromising who they were. In fact, by the 1930s, their influence was about to explode in ways that reverberate throughout South Bend today.

In a bipartisan political system, waves of immigrants created more than just neighborhoods and cultures. They created reliable voting blocs that could be wooed and exploited. As first- and second-wave Hungarians became naturalized American citizens, Democrats and Republicans both competed for their support. It was the Republicans who came out on top in the earliest salvo, earning the affections of the Hungarians with threats from factory foremen that Democratic victories would force plant closures. If those threats didn't work, plying Hungarian picnickers with alcohol would do the trick.

And while Hungarian voters weren't a pure monolith, they were loyal, reliable, organized, and active. In the years before South Bend became a lonely blue dot in an otherwise red state, the dependability of Republican Hungarian votes helped to keep the city teetering between the two parties instead of overwhelmingly in the hand of just one of them.

By 1934, the Hungarian neighborhoods had produced a bankable political star of their own. Alex Langyel was a born-and-bred Republican who first won office as the Portage Township Trustee. Langyel helped deliver South Bend for Roosevelt in 1932 and again in 1936. Given his success, charisma, and cachet, Langyel seemed to be on a fast track for the mayor's office.

But in 1942, entrenched Republican leaders voiced their opposition to Langyel's candidacy on the grounds that they didn't want an "ethnic" candidate. The move essentially froze Langyel out of the race and left him to fend for lower offices on his own.

It also upset an awful lot of Hungarians.

South Bend's Hungarians abandoned the Republican Party in droves and took their votes and organization with them. The 1942 Republican candidate was summarily trounced thanks to the help of what used to be reliable Hungarian voters. The whole affair made for a seismic shift in South Bend's precariously balanced political landscape. In the 84 years since Langyel was rejected by his own party, South Bend has had exactly two Republican mayors.

*   *   *

The Indiana Theater closed in the early 1950s. Alexander Arch passed away in 1979. As the descendants of Hungarian immigrants became more and more Americanized, Little Budapest dissolved. Instead, the children of the people who had built the neighborhood crisscrossed the country and moved to the suburbs. The Hungarian bakery closed, the goulash moved to Lydick, and the Hungarian mass at Our Lady of Hungary was replaced with a Spanish language service. In fact, the last time I stepped into that parish it was to listen my friend Michael sing in a concert celebrating the diaspora of specifically Mexican classical music.

A lot's changed in Little Budapest, but South Bend's still got a Democratic mayor, and as long as he keeps the office, the echoes of the Hungarians will continue to reverberate through the city.

CHAPTER FIVE

NO NEED TO INTRODUCE THIS GUY

A quarter-century ago, the journey into Michigan felt like an event. Michigan, after all, was a different place with different rules and customs and practices. The Michigan I remember from my youth literally existed in a different time for half of the year as Indiana maintained a stalwart refusal to observe Daylight Savings Time. In Michigan, you had to pay a deposit to buy a soda. You could sell empty cans for a nickel apiece. U-turns were legal and even encouraged. There was no need to mark the state line on most of the major roads. After all, there were liquor stores at nearly every boundary, eager to entice Hoosiers needing to violate their own state's blue laws.

But then the lines started to blur. Indiana began to spring forward and fall back. It eased up on some of its sillier laws regarding the appropriate times for the sale of alcohol. Chain stores and restaurants erased the establishments that had made both states a little more unique. With the exception of the sudden proliferation of legal dispensaries north of the state line, Indiana and Michigan flow more or less into one another with an unexciting sameness that's new for the region.

But I am convinced that there is something that is just different about Michigan, and I am sure I feel it as we pilot our bikes north across Stateline Road onto a smooth expanse of quiet bike trail. I do not know if it is the texture of the compound they use to pave the roads or the age of the trees, but there is something here that tells me we are no longer in the place we once were.

All of that said, it's not like this is some epic journey. The trip from South Bend to Niles is just about 11 miles on a bike, almost all of it on peaceful bike paths covering the flattest portions of our round earth. The trip back will be another 11 miles, but I won't be the first writer to make the commute along the river from Niles to South Bend, and I won't be the most important one either.

That's because we're stopping to see the boyhood home of Ring Lardner, a journalist and writer whose influence on American literature is almost impossible to overstate.

The house is just off the bike path and a few miles south of a downtown district that we'll have to wait to see until a little later. Lardner's home is nearing its 200th birthday and it looks pretty good for its age, its auspicious dormers and a gabled roof the only things belying its era. It wasn't the Lardners that built the home, though. That honor belongs to Rodney Paine, a

Connecticut banker who became the first mayor of Niles. In 1850, Paine built the grand Gothic house with the view of the river, never knowing that he would only be the second most famous person to call the address his home.

In many ways, it's a shame that the place is known as the Lardner House instead of the Paine Estate. After all, Rodney Paine meant more to Niles than maybe anyone else in its history, and his obituary recognizes him as such:

The death of Mr. Paine leaves vacant an honored place in the community at large. For many years he has been known by all in our midst; and he has occupied for unusual periods, positions of high honor and usefulness. As president of the then village, and afterwards mayor of the City of Niles; as member of the Common Council; as State Senator of the Commonwealth; as school director, he earned alike the respect and gratitude of his fellow citizens.

When Rodney C. Paine expired of erysipelas, Niles was left in mourning and his home would be received by a new owner. Henry and Lena Lardner – Ring's parents – purchased the place in 1875 and added a north wing to accommodate their expanding family. Ring Lardner was born inside these walls in 1885, the youngest of nine children. This was the very same home he would return to after failing out of the Armour Institute in Chicago, passing just one class. After that, Ring Lardner spent a few years trying to find his way. He floundered along several different careers, including one collecting bad debts for the Niles Gas Company (Lardner pointed out later that he'd never encountered a good one), even as his family's long-established wealth began to evaporate around him.

Of course, that's one way to describe the early life of Ring Lardner. The man himself used a different set of words to tell his autobiography, and his words, as always, were all his own:

> *Hardly a man is now alive*
> *Who cares that in March, 1885,*
> *I was born in the city of Niles,*
> *Michigan, which is 94 miles*
> *From Chicago, a city in Illinois*
> *Sixteen years later, still only a boy,*
> *I graduated from the Niles High School*
> *With a general knowledge of rotation pool.*
> *After my schooling, I thought it best*
> *To give my soul and body a rest.*

In 1905, his rest was about to be interrupted. He was just 20 years old, but Ring Lardner was about to become a superstar.

*   *   *

Edgar Stoll was the editor of the South Bend News-Times, a stubborn competitor to the long-established South Bend Tribune. Stoll had been a thorn in the side of the Tribune ever since he arrived. His paper's Democratic leanings gave him inroads in a city that would continue to move further to the political left. Stoll embraced and catered to eastern European immigrants as they continued to become more numinous in the city, running a special section each week for "News of Interest to Polish Citizens." He snagged subscribers from places that the Tribune had ignored and swiped even more from the ones the Tribune took for granted.

The South Bend News-Times maintained a long legacy of creative marketing, even making itself an early sponsor of the National Spelling Bee, long before Howard-Scripps entered the fray. The paper's first rights to report on the bee paid off in 1926, when a 13-year-old South Bender named Betty Robinson won the whole thing, correctly spelling 'albumen', or the protein of an egg white.

As the editor of South Bend's underdog newspaper, Stoll was used to poaching subscribers wherever he could find them. It was the same for writers, and that's how, in the autumn of 1905, Edgar Stoll alighted upon the doorstep of the Lardner home.

He was looking for Ring's brother, Rex, four years older and already an established writer with the Niles Daily Sun. As it happened, Rex wasn't home that day, on account of he actually had a job, so Ring entertained Stoll on his own. Through exaggerations, fictions, and a few outright lies, Ring Lardner made the case that he'd be able to do the job at least as well as his brother could. Stoll bought it, and Lardner started his new career with the South Bend News-Times the next week.

Lardner spent his first months at the News-Times covering high school sports, low-level baseball, and local amateur golf and tennis championships. His earliest pieces were mostly unremarkable and contained very little of the wit and humor that would become his trademark. All of that changed on January 1, 1907 when Lardner published a summary of the previous year in South Bend sports. Perhaps his editor was on holiday and Lardner was free to be his most authentic self. Perhaps he was trying something new just to see if it would stick. Either way, readers of the News-Times were howling with delight when they read the lede of Lardner's column:

Looking back over the past year local followers of sport have three things to be thankful for. There were no fake fights pulled off in our midst, the High school football team went through the season with no deaths and only one defeat, and the South Bend ball club did not run absolutely last.

Of course, they had no way of knowing that the words belonged to a man named Ring Larder. Journalism did not often value personality, and indeed, Lardner never received a single byline during his time at the News-Times. Still, Lardner represented something new and if the readers of the News-Times didn't take note of the man, other newspapers across the Midwest certainly did. By the end of 1907, Lardner had moved to Chicago and by 1908 he was the lead writer for the Tribune's coverage of the Chicago Cubs. His trademark humor and jovial nature ingratiated himself to the players, with a few notable exceptions; and by 1913, his columns were syndicated in more than 100 newspapers across America. Within ten years of becoming a journalist on a lark, Lardner was a household name. When the Indianapolis Star began to run Lardner's stuff ahead of the 1925 World Series, they ran his photo along with the headline, "No Need to Introduce this Guy."

It is not an overstatement to say that Ring Lardner was the most influential sportswriter of his era and perhaps the most influential sportswriter in the history American journalism. And yet, all of that would still fail to capture the incredible scope and depth of the man's impact on the written English language.

More than just a sports reporter, Lardner also accepted wartime assignments and even embedded himself into the historically epic 1924 Democratic Convention. Still the longest such gathering ever held, the Democrats tried and failed 102 times to nominate a Presidential candidate before they finally settled on John W. Davis. At one point, Lardner even earned a half-a-vote for himself after writing a satirical column offering to run. When it all ended, Lardner claimed he had predicted the outcome from the beginning, and despite the gravity of his topic, he made no attempt at comedic restraint:

If any of my readers is still living they will recall that two or three weeks ago or whenever the convention was in the throes of its infancy, I made the prediction that John W. Davis would be the nominee.

It's difficult to say what effect Lardner's coverage may have had on the eventual outcome of the election. The Democrats he covered were thoroughly trounced as Calvin Coolidge sprinted away with victory. Per-capita voter turnout for the 1924 election was – and remains – the lowest in the history of the United States. For his part, John Davis was never a candidate for any political office ever again, although he was played by Burt Lancaster in a 1991 TV film.

Lardner's interests expanded beyond the pages of the newspaper. He published more than a dozen books including fiction, satire, poetry, and compilations. His most successful work was <u>You Know Me Al</u>, a book staged as a series of letters written from the perspective of the fictional ballplayer, Jack Keefe.

But Lardner's greatest impact goes far beyond anything he created. His impression on the landscape of American literature is spelled through the absolute literary giants he inspired. Holden Caulfield famously calls Ring Lardner his "next favorite author" and if you're a reader of classic American literature, you might be surprised to learn that Ring Lardner was probably your favorite author's favorite author.

As a youngster, Ernest Hemingway used to write under the pen name *Ring Lardner, Jr.* John O'Hara credits Lardner's writing with teaching him how to write authentic dialogue. Virginia Woolf, who was never known for being a particularly funny person, called <u>You Know Me Al</u> a masterpiece. In <u>The American Language</u>, H.L. Mencken explores how the idea of common vernacular had taken hold of American literature and become one of the features that most set it apart from European writing. He gives the credit for its invention entirely to Ring Lardner:

Its discovery [the use of vernacular] had to wait until Ring Larder, a Chicago newspaper reporter. In his grotesque tales of baseball players, so immediately and so deservedly successful, Lardner reports the common speech not only with humor but with the utmost accuracy. His writings are a mine of authentic Americana; his service to etymology incomparable.

Perhaps none of his contemporaries knew the man better than F. Scott Fitzgerald, who considered Lardner a great friend and a great writer. The two met at Great Neck, on Long Island, and one imagines that upon recognizing one another's faces, they gave each other a smile with a future in it.

As pals, Fitzgerald and Lardner were inseparable. When Heart of Darkness author Joseph Conrad visited the states but refused to entertain visitors, Lardner plied Fitzgerald with alcohol and the two danced on the lawn of Conrad's rented home to try to attract the man's attention. Conrad called the police on them.

The scheme did not work, but the friendship would endure. Fitzgerald constantly encouraged his friend's writing, even as Lardner deprecated his own talents. For his part, Lardner was always supportive of Fitzgerald, even serving as an early proofreader for The Great Gatsby. Before the iconic American novel was completed, Fitzgerald had even written his friend into the book. None other than Ring Lardner was imagined as the character Owl Eyes and given the job of reciting Gatsby's obituary:

The poor son-of-a-bitch.

While F. Scott Fitzgerald was rocketing to the top of the American literary world, Lardner experienced something of his own personal literary renaissance. Although he was most known as a baseball writer, Lardner experienced a fallout with the sport in the aftermath of the 1919 Black Sox Scandal. Lardner had written extensively about both Chicago ballclubs and knew many of the players on both teams personally.

A scene in the 1988 film *Eight Men Out* even shows Lardner, portrayed by actor John Sayles, strolling through the Sox train and singing a tune. When the eight Sox players were found guilty of throwing the series and banned from the sport for life, Lardner's attitude soured toward the game and never recovered.

Instead, Lardner began to expand his repertoire into new sports and new fields including boxing, golf, politics, hard news, and theater. It was the latter that captured his interest the most, and Lardner even took up writing scripts and composing lyrics for the stage. His first Broadway success came with *Elmer, the Great*, a baseball comedy set in Lardner's wheelhouse – the titular Elmer is a slugger for the Cubs.

If *Elmer, the Great* was a play that sat firmly inside Lardner's comfort zone, his most successful play, *June Moon*, was one that took him out of it. The romantic comedy features songs and lyrics written by Lardner and has been remade and reworked for television and radio several times in the 90 years since it made its debut. Different versions of the show have included the likes of Orson Welles, Jack Benny, Jack Lemmon, Stephen Sondheim, and Sarah Jessica Parker. A 1974 television adaptation of *June Moon* helped launch the career of Susan Sarandon.

Ring Lardner was not yet 45 years old when *June Moon* made its successful run on Broadway. He was the most famous columnist in America, a best-selling author, and a successful playwright. The man was poised for a second act that might have eclipsed his first.

It never happened.

By 1931, Lardner was stricken with an illness from which he would never recover – tuberculosis. By 1933, he was dead. One of America's most important and unique voices was silenced, and a nation was left to mourn.

Lardner would have only pished and poshed at the words that were spilled in his wake. The man from Niles never thought himself much more than a silly sportswriter and a middling humorist. He would have scoffed at the idea that the middle school in his hometown would be named in his honor or that his home would make it on to the National Register of Historic Places. Lardner, as far as he was concerned, was just a man who'd been given the amazing opportunity to live his dream.

But men rarely write their own eulogies and for as many words as Lardner wrote, it was the words of his friends and admirers that would solidify his legacy. Of all of those friends, none spoke more highly of Ring Lardner than his dear friend F. Scott Fitzgerald:

A great and good American is dead. Let us not obscure him by flowers but walk up and look at that fine medallion, all abraded by sorrows that perhaps we are not equipped to understand. Ring made no enemies, because he was kind, and to many millions he gave release and delight.

CHAPTER SIX
THE DRY DITCH AND SOUTH BEND'S BRIDGE TO NOWHERE

Alexis Coquillard was a lot of different things. He was a respected agent with the American Fur Company. He was a friend to Native Americans. He was a successful trader, a respected businessman, and a well-liked community member. He was among the founding fathers of the University of Notre Dame and was the most important father of the city that would become South Bend. He was a proud American, a bold capitalist, and a generous friend.

He was not, however, a very good engineer.

A decade into his time in South Bend, Alexis Coquillard was smart enough to realize that even though the town he'd founded was built to last, the business that sustained him was about to crumble. Coquillard was well-read and well-connected, and he had the business instincts he needed to recognize when it was time to pivot. By 1835, he began to recognize the following things in order:

- The furs he traded were falling out of fashion throughout Europe and the eastern United States, even as they became harder to find and more expensive to procure.
- The Native Americans, with whom he'd established his most successful trading connections, were about to be forcibly removed, although maybe Coquillard didn't yet know that he would be the one removing them.
- Train tracks were creeping further and further east as locomotives rendered waterways like the one Coquillard controlled less and less useful for moving commerce.

So yes, things were going well with South Bend, but Coquillard had a wife and a child he had to care for, and he was well aware that the business that brought him to South Bend wouldn't be the one that kept him there.

Coquillard's family engaged in a number of business ventures in the wake of the decline of the fur trade. They opened an inn. The tavern they built is recorded as the first wooden-framed building in South Bend. Alexis Coquillard himself later opened a successful flour mill near the current location of the Century Center.

But Coquillard's most ambitious money-making attempt was the Kankakee Mill Race, a massive engineering project that would redirect the flow of the Kankakee River into the St. Joseph, promising to deliver "unlimited" hydroelectric energy to South Bend. It would be a boon for the city, and as the project's proprietor, Coquillard was poised to make a fortune off of it.

The idea was simple and seemed feasible. Coquillard was not the first to propose it, and when he finally decided to go for it, the assumption was that his plan would work. The waters of the Kankakee flowed through a place on the westside of South Bend that sat at a higher elevation than the center of downtown South Bend. All Coquillard needed to do was dig a trench between the Kankakee and the place he chose on the St. Joseph, an entry point near the corner of Riverside and Marion Streets. Profit wouldn't be far behind.

Of course, digging a four-mile ditch is a simple concept, but it's not cheap. Coquillard approached his connections at the bank, mortgaged significant land holdings, and recruited his good friend John Defrees to do the same. Armed with the investment they needed and the control over the lands they were scheduled to dig, Coquillard and Defrees got to work planning the construction of the race and began running advertisements in the papers to attract the businesses that could take advantage of it:

From the enterprise of the gentlemen who are about to erect the establishment and the un- equalled power which the union of the Kankakee and St. Joseph affords, we have no doubt but what this Mill will be equal if not superior to any similar establishment west of Rochester (N. Y.).

Coquillard and his engineers sat before a plat map of the city of South Bend and drew a meandering line that wandered northwest through the city before making an abrupt southerly turn toward what is now Beck's Lake. It wasn't the most efficient or practical race line, but it was the most economic one, designed to utilize as much of Coquillard's land as possible and then as much publicly available land as possible.

Most of his line avoided the established parts of downtown South Bend, as seizing the land would have been prohibitively expensive. But that was no matter. Once he brought infinite hydropower to a place a mile west of the center of downtown, the center of downtown would move to accommodate his creation. The Kankakee Mill Race would do more than just establish unlimited energy for South Bend; it would be cause to build a brand-new South Bend around it.

For practical reasons, the dig started at the end of the race, near the place where the waters would spill into the St. Joseph. After all, starting the dig at the beginning of the race meant that they'd constantly be contending with the flow of the water as they continued the work.

The machinery of the day was crude and prone to breakdowns. Beasts of burden were employed in just a few instances, but for the most part the work was done by men with shovels, immigrants eager to make a living and to make a mark in the new world. They didn't know it at the time, but the first thing they were going to do was to create the shape of the Near Northwest Neighborhood.

With one notable exception, there aren't many tangible reminders of the Kankakee Mill Race remaining in South Bend. But if you know where to look, there are still plenty of echoes of the line that Coquillard and his associates drew on the map. In fact, they're still drawn on the map today. Parts of Lincoln Way West were built directly atop the old Kankakee Mill Race, and the diagonal line that describes the southern border of the Near Northwest Neighborhood is directly attributable to the ditch that Coquillard and his men carved through the place in 1837.

But Coquillard and Defrees weren't in the business of neighborhood building. They knew that the race was a foolproof business proposition and were quick to acquire additional partners in the form of South Benders John Hendricks and John Rush. Additional advertisements began to fill the pages of the newspapers offering to build lots along the new Kankakee Mill Race. Coquillard would be making a lot of men – men besides himself – rich with his business venture.

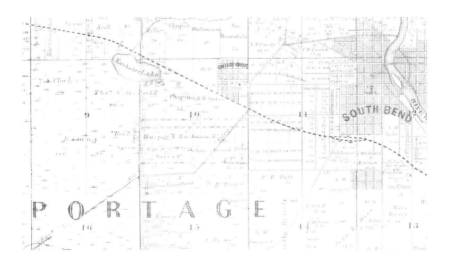

At a place near Blaine Street, Coquillard's laborers carved a southerly turn into the race, directing a path toward and through the South Bend City Cemetery. The ditch dodged the handful of tombstones that had already been laid, and a crude stone bridge was erected to deliver mourners from one side of the cemetery to the other. It would become one of dozens of bridges crews built to help pedestrians navigate and cross the Kankakee Mill Race.

Today, behind rows of well-manicured stones that bear many of the same names as the streets that make up the downtown grid, the bridge in the graveyard is still standing, and it's a bridge that doesn't need to exist. It's an adorable feature of the historic cemetery; a useless bridge that connects nothing to nowhere, that safely moves travelers from one side of one grassy field to another. The ditch that ran below that bridge has been filled for a century-and-a-half. If humans weren't a sentimental people, the bridge would have been removed a long time ago. Over the course of the past 150 years, dozens like it already have been.

Once the ditch was dug through and past the cemetery, the builders executed a west turn at the place that is now the parking lot of Frankie's BBQ. Another whisper of the Kankakee Mill Race is heard at the corner of West Washington Street and Circle Avenue. The bend here in Washington Street was another accommodation to the race that would run due west for the remainder of its journey toward Beck's Lake.

Once considered to be a part of the headwaters of the Kankakee River, Beck's Lake has experienced an eclectic and tragic history since the years when it was the chief aim of Coquillard's scheme to provide unlimited power to the city of South Bend. In the early 1900s, when the Kankakee was dredged, there was some amount of surprise that Beck's Lake wasn't drained by the process. Indeed, larger and more significant lakes were left empty by dredging operations across the state.

Somehow, Beck's Lake remained.

It might have been a miracle.

But it wasn't.

In fact, it might have been better for generations of South Benders if the lake had been demolished the way the rest of the Grand Kankakee Marsh was.

In the years that followed, businesses[7] began to use Beck's Lake as a community dumping ground for toxic waste. Once upon a time, the land around Beck's Lake was the only place in South Bend where African Americans were allowed to build and buy homes. The whole time, the soil beneath their feet was chockfull of asbestos, lead, and arsenic. In the 1950s, the city turned the land into a public park, and in 1984, Bendix came forward to inform the city of their dumping activities, nearly 50 years after the fact. By 2013, the EPA declared Beck's Lake to be one of the most contaminated sites in America. In 2022, massive remediation efforts sought to correct a decades-old problem, more than 70 years too late for the families who had lived – and died prematurely – on the land around the lake.

---

[7] Studebaker and Oliver were among those who used Beck's Lake as a dumping ground, but the worst offender – by far – was Bendix. Beck's Lake sits less than half-a-mile from the old Bendix production grounds and was a convenient place for the company to dump paint, solvents, and heavy metals. Although Studebaker and Oliver are firmly out of business, Bendix was sold once, sold again, and remains an active business. Its current owners, Honeywell, struck a deal to assist with cleanup costs of Beck's Lake, but did not admit any liability.

But when Coquillard's ditch approached the lake, the waters were still clean, still fed by and feeding into the Kankakee River. The waters provided reason for optimism. Months of labor had all been leading toward the moment when the final shovelfuls of dirt would be removed and the waters would begin filling the ditch, racing toward the St. Joseph River, and creating something like a brand-new river through the city of South Bend.

The work had only gotten easier as Coquillard's hired hands approached the lake. The rich soil became softer and more forgiving, and the men's spirits soared as their pace quickened and the promise of completion became more tangible.

The historical record is sparse with the details, but one has to imagine that Coquillard was present for the moment. Perhaps he even manned the shovel himself. Perhaps he saw the few inches of loose sail standing between his dry ditch and the promise of wealth and riches contained in the waters of the Kankakee. Coquillard was a devout Catholic. Indeed, he was an early champion of the founding of the University of Notre Dame; so it is not unreasonable to suspect that the man whispered a prayer before in the moments before the dig was complete.

The prayer didn't work.

The water didn't flow.

It was taken back by the loose soil, filtered back into the earth by sandy dirt and once underground, returned toward Beck's Lake. The whole process was inevitable and ordained by the laws of nature. Coquillard had tried to carve a race and build a river through a watershed. In fact, rainwater that drained into the race tended to run west toward Beck's Lake, instead of toward the St. Joseph, the way it was supposed to.

After spending thousands and thousands of dollars (that he didn't really have) to dig the canal and span it with bridges like the one in the cemetery, Coquillard must have watched with trembling disappointment as the water refused to move. There wasn't even a trickle of water from one river that moved into another.

But Alexis Coquillard was not a man who gave up easily. In truth, he was prone to the occasional boast about his stubbornly earned successes, bragging that he had once gone to court against President Martin Van Buren and come out on top. Recounting the victory, he wrote to a friend:

As you can see I have wiped out great men.

But Coquillard was also a man who was prone to failing spectacularly. In 1842, he commissioned a boat builder to build him a vessel that could deliver tons of flour all the way to Lake Michigan. After a significant outpouring of cost, the ship – named the *South Bend* managed one voyage – before being put to rest after failing the journey. In the case of the Kankakee Mill Race, Coquillard would either win or he would go up in flames. There would be no in-between. He'd already constructed two of his own mills along the course of the race by the time the waters had failed to flow.

Coquillard doubled down, ordering new drawings, new constructions, and new engineerings. Further attempts to solve the problem with a bulwark dam were utterly fruitless, but what they lacked in results, they made up for in their price tag. By 1840, there was no choice but to abandon the venture and eat the cost.

The dry ditch was an eyesore in South Bend for the next several decades and provided none of the benefits it had promised to deliver. Newspaper reports from 1883 indicate that the race had turned into a dumping spot for the city's refuse. There was even a lawsuit filed after an accumulation of junk formed a makeshift dam in front of James Batchellor's home and flooded his property when rainwater spilled into his yard.

As for men behind the venture, Defrees was bankrupted entirely. The entire incident would come to be known as Coquillard's Folly, but maybe a better name would have been Coquillard's Foreclosure, because that's what happened next. After defaulting on his loans, Coquillard watched helplessly as his land was seized by the bank. The failure was bad for Coquillard and his cohorts, but it would prove to be very good for the bank:

The [bank] had purchased a large amount of the personal paper of Alexis Coquillard, which on the failure of the... Kankakee mill race, this paper became quite valueless as bank assets... Some 2,479 acres... eventually came into the possession of the bank by foreclosure and was sold to great advantage and profit to the stockholders.

The Near West Side (or West Washington) neighborhood was born from Coquillard's foreclosures, and in fact; the original land deeds still refer to the area as the "Bank Outlot Subdivision." Today, this neighborhood is home to some of the grandest and most famous homes in all of South Bend. In a strange way, it's both fitting and poetic that the most historic homes in the city sit atop the land that used to belong to its founder.

Joseph Bartlett's Home at 720 West Washington was the first of these and would go on to become (if the stories are true) a stop on the Underground Railroad. Later, the Olivers would build Copshaholm in the Bank Outlot Subdivision and the Studebakers would build Tippecanoe Place; monuments to proud and wealthy families, all constructed on the land that used to be Alexis Coquillard's. It's the same place the History and Studebaker Museums sit today.

In the years that followed, the failed race would continue to fuel controversy and conspiracy. Although the ditch is filled and covered now, it's a valid historical question to wonder what exactly they filled it with. Rumors abounded that police had broken up illegal casinos, seized property, and smashed gaming tables to bits before depositing them in the ditch that ran through the City Cemetery. During Prohibition, there were rumors that liquor stills were destroyed and deposited in the same way.

If there's any truth to the conspiracy, then it seems likely that there are more than just bodies buried at the City Cemetery, but we'll probably never know for sure. Radar technologies that scan for the presence of underground metals have proved inconclusive, and although construction work along the old race turned up metal parts of some contraption or another, it's not like they're going to excavate the most historic cemetery in South Bend just to track down a few busted slot machines. If the Babe Ruth bat that I've been hunting for half a year is down there, I'm almost certainly never going to find it.

In the meantime, it's worth a visit to the South Bend City Cemetery to check out Alexis Coquillard's bridge to nowhere. After all, it might just be the only collection of stones in the historic graveyard with nothing important underneath it.

CHAPTER SEVEN

ALL HAIL THE HUCKLEBERRY QUEEN

It's a non-descript bike ride to the south from Walkerton, first rolling beyond the bounds of St. Joseph County, and then turning east toward the unimpressively unincorporated community of Tyner, Indiana. It's a place pockmarked with farmlands and interspersed with nothingness, the kind of location whose presence on Google is labeled with a photograph that tells a thousand words:

There's nothing *wrong* with Tyner, of course. It's just not the kind of place that feels terribly notable. It's the kind of town you'd drive through without ever realizing you'd driven through a town because you hadn't just driven through a town. You'd passed a Methodist church, a shuttered grocery store, and a company that may or may not deal in steel. Down the road there's a golf course, and that's as exciting as Tyner gets.

But 150 years ago, at least during the later parts of the humid wetland summers, when the swamp plants came into their fullest portion of bloom, Tyner might have been the most exciting place in the entire world, and there are plenty of stories and characters to help prove it.

The long-expired marshlands of northern Indiana birthed life and lives long forgotten, stories of animals extincted, biomes evaporated, and climates changed and erased. For a while, the muddy marshes of Tyner, Indiana were among the most legendary of these wetlands, launching communities and economies, churches and orgies, criminals and evangelists.

Wild huckleberries grew almost without limit in the damp underbrush of Tyner's Great Huck Marsh, inviting a crowd of itinerant laborers to comb through a thousand acres of marshland to harvest the swampy crop. Tyner exploded during the summers when the huckleberries came into season. As many as 5,000 people spilled into the marsh to pick huckleberries, wallow in the mud, and drink to – and beyond – their fill.

It was an eclectic collection of the furthest flung fringes of 1870's society – circus acts, carnival workers, gamblers, irreligious rejects, gypsies, hoboes, vagrants, pre-Marxists, hooch enthusiasts, pickpockets, scam artists, pagans, hardened criminals and low-grade thieves, backwoods musicians with accordions and cymbals, traveling magicians and dealers of potions, post-capitalist utopian wannabes, fortune tellers, treasure hunters, revelers, rabble-rousers, refugees, runaways, prostitutes and their keepers, early progressive first-wave hippies, post-racial harmonists, desperadoes, ritualists, dancers with tassels and bobbles, disinterested degenerate distillers, anarchists, early overdosers, exploiters of cheap labor, ambitious voodoo entrepreneurs, conspiracy theorists, failed politicians, snake oil druggists, and of course, the veritable army of committed protestant preachers bound and determined to save all of them from their sin.

Each summer, the more industrious itinerants would arrive just ahead of the season in order to erect hasty shelters for themselves along the edges of the swampland. The less sedulous arrived along with the huckleberries and would camp in the mud for the length of their stay. It was no matter. For many of the berry farmers, the places they lived weren't as important as the places they would party. Instead of building primitive homes, they placed their efforts into more rewarding endeavors, constructing dance floors, gaming tables, roughshod bar tops, hooch stills, slot machines, and makeshift brothel tents.

It was a debaucherous party, but it was also a lucrative one. According to The Plymouth Democrat in 1870:

The huckleberry trade is enormous. Shipment of huckleberries from Marshall County often exceeded 200 bushels per day in August. Prices range from $1.50 to $3.00 per bushel…

Adjusting for inflation, the vagrants of the Great Huck Marsh were pushing nearly $15,000 a day in huckleberries. For the unskilled and uneducated, their daily profits dwarfed what they might receive in more traditional endeavors, but they wouldn't keep much of the money themselves. Instead, they passed most of their profits along to drink-pourers, card-dealers, and women of the night.

It's difficult to know how many of the thousands were actively working the swamp to harvest the huckleberries, how many were there to provide their own illicit services to the laborers, and how many were there only to partake in those same illicit services. The work drove the nightlife and the nightlife became its own tourist attraction. The renown of the marsh spilled across the nation and its tawdry scandals were told in newspapers as far afield as Colorado, New York, Florida, Nebraska, and Washington state:

Pickpockets, thieves, and strumpets mingle among the pickers... Gambling, drinking, violence, and prostitution are carried on to a fearful extent... There are 500 fallen women there on Sundays... no exaggeration.

For some time, the chaos that drew them there was the same chaos that ruled and policed the marsh, the demands of the place too big for the quiet precincts monitored by the part-time sheriffs in neighboring counties. Brawls and drunken fights resulted in gouged eyes, ripped ears, indiscriminate shootings, and even a handful of deaths. Left to its own devices, perhaps the marsh would have destroyed itself, or maybe the preachers would have saved it. Instead, the marsh took it upon itself to appoint a leader.

The place had been an anarchy.

It was about to become a monarchy.

*   *   *

No one really knows how Mary Louisa came to arrive at the Great Huck Marsh. According to one account, she came simply because she wanted to ride the carousel that had been erected by a Michigan City businessman. Others claim that she was a circus performer who worked under the alias, "The Woman with the Iron Jaw" and that she was there to put on a show. Less generous narratives peg her as a prostitute out of an Indianapolis outfit who was willing to travel and compromise her working conditions in exchange for a little bit of extra pay.

The details of her life are sketchy at best. Mary Louisa was sometimes a mystery, always an enigma, and hallowed as a legend. By 1879, she was the subject of a biography, and while I am loath to cast unfounded aspersions on the journalistic credibility of the long deceased, I would be remiss if I did not mention that the author of the book, Adalbert Knott[8], did deliberately choose a headshot for himself that answers the question, "What if all three of the Stooges managed to have a child together?"

---

[8] Knott would go on to become an actor of middling renown, appearing on Broadway and in many early Hollywood films, including *Big Stakes* and *The Brat*.

There are but a handful of details about Mary Louisa's early life that are generally agreed upon – that she loved liquor and cigars, that she'd led a rough-and-tumble life, and that she was blonde, beautiful, and impressively buxom. Given all that, there were any number of reasons the woman might have chosen the marsh, but in the end, none of the theories hold up.

That's because Mary Louisa didn't choose the marsh.

The marsh chose her.

From the moment she arrived in the wetlands, Mary Louisa was a sensation. Whether it was the dynamite force of her massive personality, her professional prowess, or some strange magic of the long-expired marshlands; the people of the place flocked to the new woman who would come to call the wetlands her home and perhaps even her fiefdom:

When she went to the marsh, her strength, dash and utter abandon won her, by common consent, the title of 'Huckleberry Queen' and not one dare dispute it. She reigns supreme over the marsh.

In her own way, Mary Louisa became the moral compass of the Great Huck Marsh, dealing roguish justice swiftly and without the benefit of due process. She made short work of men accused of rape, beating them senseless, and then dismissing them entirely. Legends told stories of the Queen saving men from drowning, providing food for the hungry, and procuring medicine for sick women.

And yet, the Huckleberry Queen was far from angelic. She wielded her power in wicked demonstrations, once whipping her own husband in sight of the masses as a show of her own strength and discompassion. It was known throughout the marsh that the Queen's power and temper were far greater than her benevolence, once tracking a practical joker far outside the boundaries of the marsh to whip him in the street for his insolence. She was a regular in local papers and a headline writers' waking dream:

A Bourbonite Was Skilleted Over the Head by the Huckleberry Queen on Saturday

For the duration of the Queen's reign, the marsh had law even if it did not have order. Mary Louisa's rule was absolute, and when the debauchery spilled onto certain private lands, even those landowners did not question her authority. Instead, the Huckleberry Queen negotiated with well-to-do and upstanding landowners throughout the Great Huck Marsh. In return for tolerating the revelers and turning a blind eye to the debauchery, she would guarantee they received profits from the crop harvested on their land. It wasn't a bad deal, and it was certainly better than being on the wrong end of the Queen's ire.

The legend of the Huckleberry Queen only continued to grow throughout the 1870s. The National Police Gazette ran an article in August 1879 that called the Queen a notorious harlot so bad that whenever a rattlesnake bites her, the rattlesnake dies.

But it turns out that not everyone was a fan of the diaspora of humanity that called the marsh its home for eight weeks every year. Not everyone was a fan of their Queen either:

The movement of the citizens of St. Joe, Starke and Marshall to secure law and order on the marshes near here meets the hearty approval of the citizens of Walkerton and surrounding country, as gambling, selling and drinking lightning whiskey and fighting and raising the associations of hell generally are always carried on to a frightful extent at the ephemeral city that springs up every year. By the vigorous use of all the lawful means within our power we shall assuredly rescue our fair name and our borders from deep dishonor and sickening contamination of this foul cesspool whose offense is rank and smells to heaven!

For years, attempts by outsiders to enforce laws and morality upon the denizens of the marsh had proved fruitless. In the end, it would prove unnecessary.

Saddened by the sin she'd seen her son succumb to, an incensed mother marched into the marsh at season's end, doused the whole thing with kerosene, and burned it all down. During the next decade, efforts to drain northern Indiana's marshlands would ensure that none of it would ever come back. The acres were recovered, restored, and replanted as celery fields, and if you're thinking that the coronation of a Celery Queen doesn't quite have the same ring to it, you're exactly right. Woodstock was over and when it was over, it wasn't coming back ever again.

And yet, despite the moralistic victory the region would celebrate over the end of the debaucherous reign of the Huckleberry Queen, there was a pervasive sense that something unique and important had been lost. As for the Queen, she was reduced to a hovel in Valparaiso, and by 1902 she was dying, no doubt a result of her rough living.

The newspapers eulogized and remembered her differently, some as a low-level anarchist warlord and others as a sideshow or passing fascination. Some papers recognized her as something that mattered, as a person who, if she did not make north-central Indiana better, at least made it more interesting. For as much as some of them hated her, they had no choice but to admit that the Huckleberry Queen was nothing if not fascinating:

St. Joseph County, the hitherto undisputed realm of that patron saint of morality, the Huckleberry Queen, is to lose a distinction it has possessed for years and years. The big huckleberry marsh, which occupied a great share of the county and was known throughout this and adjoining states and which has in time past produced such immense crops of berries and criminals, is to be converted into a peaceful celery garden by the owner. What will become of her huckleberry majesty to whose despotic sway her subjects bowed humbly, or the subjects themselves, is largely a matter of conjecture; but they will doubtless succeed in finding green fields and pastures new, where the regular summer orgies and bouts can be continued uninterruptedly by the interfering hand of the law. We'll all miss them but to old St. Joe county, the loss will be doubly heavy.

HELL IS A PLACE NOT FAR FROM GRANGER, INDIANA

No one knows how the town of Hell, Michigan got its name, and after my wife and I rode our bikes there from South Bend, we're no closer to finding an answer. My favorite theory is that the founder of the town was asked what he wanted to name the place and he responded, "Name it Hell for all I care!"

Whatever the reason, at some point I settled on the idea that we should go to Hell. It had been suggested to me several times before during bike rides, usually by impatient motorists with middle fingers extended from car windows.

So I pitched the idea to my wife, Ashley. We could ride bikes for some 330 miles over the course of Independence Day weekend, and in so doing, we would be able to claim that we'd been to Hell and back.

"Do we have time to train for that?" she asked.

"Yes," I lied.

*　　*　　*

And so it came time for us to embark on our adventure with almost no training miles under our belts, and a few too many cheeseburgers under mine. It was the end of June, Canada was on fire, and the Midwest was covered in a smoky dystopian haze. We were on our way to Hell. It only made sense.

We packed up our things, and I nagged Ashley and then nagged her again to see if she was ready yet.

"Go to Hell," she smiled.

We rolled out on a blazing hot St. Joseph County day. I'd been following the weather at home and at all of our stayover towns and knew things were much more temperate up north at our final destination.

"Hotter than Hell down here," I pointed out.

Our route took us east along the state line, bouncing back and forth between Indiana and Michigan until we reached Mottville and stayed in the Wolverine state for good. Mottville is notable as the hometown of pitcher Harvey Freeman, who spent one year in the big leagues and compiled a 1-4 record with a 7.69 ERA. As a hitter he went 1-for-12 during his only campaign.

It's not an impressive stat line, but it's more hits and more wins than anyone who drinks beer with me on a regular basis has. Later in his life, Freeman would become a legendary Michigan high school basketball coach, winning five championships with Kalamazoo from 1925-1954.

It took longer to tell that story than it took us to ride through Mottville and get that much closer to Hell.

Mottville gave way to Constantine, home of renowned WW1 Major General Harry Hill Bandholtz, a man who is now honored with a statue in Budapest. Constantine gave way to Centreville, home of renowned actor Verne Troyer, who you best know as Mini Me from the Austin Powers movies.

It was on a bench in Centrevillle that we became party to a raucous courthouse wedding in which everyone's dogs were invited and both brides may have steadily smoked Marlboro Reds through the ceremony. It was too bad we couldn't stick around, but then, Hell waits for no man.

At some point before we stumbled into the town of Colon, we found ourselves riding alongside the Colon Ditch. Dear reader, please know that I am only trying to deliver as much factual accuracy as I can when I relay to you that the Colon Ditch is a backed-up flow of muddy water that spills through a narrow pipe and into a lake.

The town of Colon is known as The Magic Capital of the World and remains home to some of the most prestigious illusion shoppes in the world. The town is decorated with statues of magician's rabbits, and the town's high school mascot is probably something magician-adjacent, but I can't rule out that they may also be called the Polyps.

A left turn poured us onto a narrow one-lane road that would prove to be our exit from Magic City. Ashley and I managed to push our way through the center of Colon before being squeezed out of the back, left to go our own way from now on.

That's when the cramps started to set in. Our feet, backs, stomachs, and hamstrings started to seize, leaving us on the side of sweltering roads doing impromptu yoga routines and yelling about wiggling our toes. At least twice my right thumb cramped and froze, and that wasn't even a thing that I knew could happen.

97

We were only halfway to our final destination and everything was about to go to Hell.

The going was slow, the heat was oppressive, and for the first time, the roads were beginning to work against us. The final run-in to Battle Creek was pockmarked with gravel and potholes, less a roadway than an obstacle course designed to punish a cyclist's most sensitive bits.

Somehow we arrived at the hotel. I went to check us in. The woman at the desk smiled a friendly smile.

Then she spoke:

"Our hotel is actually being shut down because we don't have any water. I can tell you that the nearest hotels with occupancy are in Kalamazoo."

"How far away is that?"

"About 30 miles give or take."

"Oof."

Long story short, I was much relieved to learn that I had taken us to the wrong hotel and that our actual destination was a little further down the road. The real hotel had water. We ate burritos and milkshakes before making final preparations for our arrival in Hell. The next day was going to be worse than this one:

"Hell from beneath is excited about you, To meet you at your coming; It stirs up the dead for you, All the chief ones of the earth; It has raised up from their thrones All the kings of the nations." ~ Isaiah 14:9

The morning was cloudy and humid, and it seemed like a harbinger of things to come when the shoulders of the roadways were immediately littered with dead skunks. It wasn't the sulfuric odor I'd long associated with Biblical interpretations of the road to Hell, but it was pretty bad. On the plus side, the weather was cooler than it had been the day before and promised to remain that way for the duration of our journey.

Our first stop of the day came on a sad bench at a sad park outside Marshall. Marshall is home to Mythbuster Jamie Hyndman; former NFL Head Coach Adam Gase; and most exciting of all, an 1800s surveyor named Sam Hill whose propensity for profanity was so famous that his own name became a substitute for curse words, as in: "What the Sam Hill?"

But we didn't come this far to settle for a euphemism. We came for the real thing. Hell was just up the road and for a while I was sure I could smell it, but it was just another dead skunk.

Next came a stop at a gas station in Albion, the hometown of deadball era catcher Deacon McGuire, a true revolutionary in the game of baseball. McGuire was the first man to add padding to his catcher's mitt, doing so by stuffing a raw steak into the palm of the glove before each game. The innovation helped lengthen McGuire's career, and over the course of 26 seasons, he threw out 1,459 would-be base stealers, which remains a major league record.

As we continued to ride through the thick humidity, I became keenly aware that the padding of my bike shorts was caked with a potent blend of road grime, sweat, farts, skunk residue, and smoke advisories. I did take some solace in knowing that none of me could possibly smell worse than Deacon McGuire's glove at the end of an August doubleheader.

It's at the town of Parma that I noticed a billboard with a proud can of Busch Light staged against a mountain and a stream accompanied with environmental ad copy:

"Protect. Restore. Conserve."

I find this ironic because I know that empty cans of Busch Light are the single most littered item on midwestern country roads. It's so bad that we've made a game out of it, counting cans of Busch Light on a bike ride the same way that you might count Volkswagens or yellow cars on a road trip. It's not because Busch Light is the most popular beer in the Midwest - it isn't. But it is the most popular beer among the demographic of people who are willing to openly drink in their cars and then pitch their empties out the window when they're done.

I've oft heard it said that the road to Hell is paved with good intentions, but I think it might be more accurate to say that the road to Hell is dotted with empty cans of Busch Light and a truly disproportionate number of festering skunk corpses.

The next waypoint on the road to Hell was Jackson, Michigan; hometown of Jack Paar, Tony Dungy, and James Earl Jones. We saw none of those people while we waited out a hailstorm at the library. I checked the weather. It was raining in Jackson, but all dry a little further east.

"Wetter than Hell down here," I pointed out.

We steeled our nerve for the last part of the journey and pointed ourselves due northeast along a crushed gravel path through a collection of apocalyptic gnats and mosquitoes that seemed appropriate as the final guardians on the way to Hell. We stopped briefly for a snack in Stockbridge, which is home to no famous people, and then we were on our way at long last. There was no turning back.

I've been apprised before of man's long descent into Hell, but if you're coming from the west, it's actually a climb. A few ups and downs, a few winding roads, and then we were there. We'd made it.

We were in Hell.

And Hell was… underwhelming.

There were a few small shoppes, some clever signs, and groups of bikers (bikers, not cyclists) celebrating the long weekend at the Hell Saloon. We took a selfie:

And then we left.

Turns out there are no hotels in Hell.

So we rolled another 15 miles further south through unexpected detours and around unexpectedly unpaved roads before we arrived in Chelsea, Michigan (home of Jeff Daniels!).

When we planned this trip, I told Ashley we'd ride 75 miles per day. By the time I showed her the day's route, it was 85 miles. By the time we finished the day, we were at 95 miles. I asked if she wanted to do another five so we could get to a hundred.

"Go to Hell," she smiled again.

*   *   *

In 2008, I attempted a cross-country bikepacking trip with my best friend Paul. We got across Wisconsin and Minnesota before making our way into North Dakota, where Paul ended up at a hospital in a town called Devil's Lake. We ended up stuck there for a few days until we could get a train back to Chicago.

So when we woke up on the third day of this Hell trip to news of severe thunderstorms that would keep us in Hell all day, it wasn't the first time I'd been stranded on a bikepacking trip in a town with a Satanic name.

Fortunately for us, we do have friends, and Hell really isn't that far from Granger, Indiana. Our friend Jen agreed to rescue us from Hell and to bring us safely home, which is roughly the plot of the 1998 film *What Dreams May Come*, in which Robin Williams and Cuba Gooding Jr. descend into the underworld to rescue Williams' suicided wife from her eternal torment. I watched that movie on a date with a girl when I was 17 and she asked me if I would do the same thing for her someday if I had to. It was our second date, and based on my answer to her question, it was also our last date.

The truth is, there are not many people who I'd be willing to go to Hell for, but I'm fortunate enough to have someone who would go to Hell for me. From the beginning, this whole harebrained scheme was woefully under planned, under resourced, and under trained. But Ashley went for it anyway, no questions asked.

It's good to have someone who's up for an adventure anywhere, anytime, and for any reason without complaint or reservation.

Even when I put her through Hell.

CHAPTER EIGHT
WHEN WE GET TO CHRISTIANA CREEK

If you know where to look, the echoes of an incredible history are preserved all around Cass County. Old homes with hidden attics straddle well-trod country roads, once among the final whistle stops along the Underground Railroad. Aging churches with important graveyards remember a racial harmony that was unique for its time and unique in the nation. Historical markers commemorate some of the finest battles that were ever fought by the otherwise peaceful Quakers.

But if you don't know where to look, you might not ever know that any of it was ever there. Instead, you might see the tattered confederate flag that riffles through the breeze in the distance, above an equally tattered home, occupying what was once a rich farmland carefully and painstakingly cleared by hardworking African American pioneers more than a century ago. Generations of escaped slaves risked life and limb so that they wouldn't have to live beneath the tyranny of everything the flag represented, and now it flies above their cemeteries, watching them in death.

The faded flag is a symbol that flies in defiance or ignorance of everything that happened here before, a symbol that wants to erase and destroy, that wants to denigrate the families and individuals who built the place from scratch. Even the whipping wind seems intent on removing the thing from its flagpole, and for my part, I am rooting for the wind. The dilapidated meter of filthy cloth keeping watch over the dirty yard is a symbol that could not more oppositely represent the legacy of its township. In truth, it most accurately represents everything that the earliest pioneers of the region had overcome. The bedraggled banner is nothing more than a loser's logo, a symbol that wants to persuade us to pretend that none of it ever happened, a symbol that peddles in willful stupidity, and one that absolutely does not want you to read this chapter of this book.

Read on.

*   *   *

The story begins in 1836 when a group of southern Quakers relocated to Cass County, citing their stringent abolitionist values. They had spoken openly about the evils of slavery, but realized that their participation in an economy built on the back of slave labor was to be complicit in its practice.

So they left.

But for the Carolina Quakers, it wasn't quite so easy. Carolina law maintained that freed slaves could be captured and returned to slavery, and indeed, there became a cottage industry in the recapturing of human beings who'd been set free by their masters. Many of the Carolina Quakers took toward buying up those slaves and providing them as free a life as possible without exposing them to the potential horrors of a resale.

The only problem, then, was that to leave Carolina for moral reasons meant leaving their slaves behind to an unknown fate. So when they left, they offered to bring the slaves with them. The first to leave was a white Quaker preacher named Henry Way. He moved to Calvin Township in Cass County and brought with him a freed slave named Lawson. Other Quakers would follow, sneaking word into southern slave communities that they were moving to southern Michigan, and that there would be home and opportunity for African Americans who could find their way there.

The echoes of the Quaker fathers of Cass County of the place ring out along roads with names like Penn and Dutch

106

Settlement. And while they never forgot their promise to build a land of opportunity for their African American brothers and sisters, there was something else that needed to be built first. They needed a church.

Stephen Bogue was among the more prominent early Quakers in Cass County. His home near Diamond Lake was the busiest stop on the Cass County line of the Underground Railroad and the first unofficial house of worship for the area's Quaker community. They would build and rebuild new and larger houses of worship every few years, but each was sparse and spartan. After all, having a community home was important, but doing the work of the community was moreso.

By 1850, Cass County was a final destination along the Underground Railroad for many escaped slaves and a forever home for many freed ones. The Quakers of Cass County had kept to their word, offering land, friendship, and opportunity to anyone who would choose to call Cass County their home. And when they needed to, the Quakers went one step further in their hospitality.

Despite their stringent commitment to pacifism, the Quakers offered their protection. It wasn't a hypocrisy, nor was it a betrayal of their values. They simply valued abolition even more than they valued non-violence.

In 1847, when 30 armed men arrived from Kentucky to take back their escaped slaves, more than 300 Cass County residents were there at O'Dell's Mill on Christiana Creek to take on the fight. Perry Sanford was one of the slaves they had come for, and he remembered the night this way:

"That was one of the most exciting anti-slavery events that ever happened in Michigan. They came down in a body and captured nearly all the slaves in that section. You see, the slave owners knew this Quaker settlement and they knew it was headquarters for escaped slaves. They brought tobacco wagons with them in which to carry back the fugitives."

The slave catchers spent a few days in prison on charges of trespassing and disturbing the peace, but that was just the beginning of the drawn out legal process. Fearful that the trial wouldn't go their way, many of the freed slaves who'd been targeted chose to move away, mostly toward Battle Creek and into Canada. The bounty hunters were released one-by-one under shady conditions, and then the litigation began. In the end, none of the slaves were extradited back to Kentucky, although some of the Michiganders did end up paying restitution in court. They all agreed that it was a small price to pay to guarantee the freedom of their fellow man, and as for the slave catchers:

"They went home an awfully disgusted and mad crowd. They didn't take their old tobacco wagons back with them. Every morning, a wheel would be missing from those wagons, until every one had disappeared. Those wheels are now resting peacefully in the bottom of Diamond Lake."

The incident made the national news, drawing the ire of southern slaveholders and the admiration of many African Americans looking for an opportunity they could call their own. After all, very rarely did freedom mean anything like equality, and sometimes even freedom led back to bondage all over again. By their actions, the Quakers of Cass County showed that they were committed to a racial equality far beyond its time and well beyond abolitionism. It had begun with a handful of disgusted white Quakers and a few freed slaves, but now it had become a nationally known antebellum black haven.

Southern slaves began to hum a new song to themselves when they dreamed of their freedom: *When We Get to Christiana Creek*. They came in droves, and when they finally arrived in Cass County, it must have seemed too good to be true. They were welcomed with open arms by white Quakers and supported by free blacks who could commiserate with their own similar journey.

That's not to say that life was easy. It wasn't. For people who'd lived their entire lives in the deep south, contending with a frigid Michigan winter was a challenge unto itself. And even with the help of their neighbors, clearing mature forest and terraforming it into suitable farmland was a backbreaking labor at best. It was hard work. But it was real freedom, and just as importantly, it was real opportunity.

By 1860, tiny Cass County held Michigan's largest African American population outside of Detroit. More than 100 of them lived in a peculiar settlement called Ramptown, named after a wild vegetable that grew in the area. The settlement grew and thrived on land belonging to James Bonine, and included 20-30 cabins, a church, and a school. Ramptown was a last stop for travelers on the Underground Railroad and the first stop in building a free life. Bonine housed the African Americans of Ramptown and paid them a fair wage in exchange for their labor. After a year or two, most of Ramptown's residents had saved enough money to purchase their own land and to start their own farms. You wouldn't know it to look upon the impressive Bonine home today, but its backyard used to hold an entire African American town.

To call all of this unique would be an understatement. Even after the Emancipation Proclamation and in the aftermath of the Civil War, there were few places where blacks stood on anything like equal footing with their white neighbors. Sharecropping ruled the south. Segregation-based power dynamics ruled everywhere else. But in Cass County, and especially in Calvin Township, African Americans were proving that all they'd ever needed was an opportunity.

Cornelius Lawson was a descendant of the first freed slave to call Cass County his new home. By 1898, he was elected the Supervisor of the Township of Calvin. A few years later, Abner Byrd would be elected Town Clerk and Matthew Artis would win a position as Treasurer.

It's an amazing thing to consider today, because while there's nothing particularly wrong with Cass County, it doesn't strike you as a place that holds uniquely progressive race relations. That's because it's not. Just five percent of the county's population is African American. Only one of their elected officials is. The Confederate Flag I noted at the beginning of the chapter is far from the only one I've seen flying along the backroads of Cass County and most of the roads are backroads. But by the late 1800s, if there was one place in the United States where the American Dream could be made a reality for African Americans, it was in Cass County, Michigan.

By 1904, the rural enclave of Calvin Township held more black families than white ones, and more often than not, the African Americans were the more prosperous of the bunch. Surprisingly, this disparity did not seem to sow much in the way of discord between the groups, and according to the existing history of the area, race relations were far more positive than not.

It was a unique situation that drew the attention of researchers and activists from around the nation. Even among some abolitionists, there were questions about whether the slaves, once freed, had the capacity to thrive in a free and modern society. It was the mission of Booker T. Washington to prove that they could. Cass County would become his case study for the nation.

Washington reported that Calvin Township first came to his attention during a visit to South Bend where he offered effusive praise toward the Studebaker family for their progressivism in race relations.[9] When the Studebakers passed along word of the black settlement just north of the state line in Calvin Township, Washington was intrigued. When the Studebakers further pointed out that they often sold wagons on

---

[9] It's worth pointing out that Washington was visiting Studebaker during its early days, when it was still the premier builder of wagons in the United States. Much of progress the early Studebaker factory made in race equality would evaporate with future regimes, and the experience of black autoworkers did not align with what Washington described this way: "The firm had never permitted any color line to be drawn in any department of their works."

credit to those same blacks, who proved just as reliable, trustworthy, and prompt as their white neighbors; he knew he had to visit the place for himself:

"I had always been anxious to see just what progress in self-government any large number of people of my race could make when left absolutely to themselves and given the advantage of the climate and location that the average white man in America possesses."

Washington stepped into a carriage alongside the county's judge, a local newspaperman, and a prosperous African American farmer. Over the course of ten hours along the same Cass County country roads that I have traversed hundreds of times on bicycle, Washington noted impressive farms and well-kept homes. He even went out of his way to note that the home-cured pork he tried was the best he ever tasted.

Of course, Booker T. Washington was not surprised to see African Americans thriving in Cass County. As an activist, he would have expected to find the same success anywhere that his kinsmen would have been given half-an-opportunity. But he also knew he was writing for a skeptical audience.

Washington iterates that the African Americans of Cass County were up to the standard of their white peers in terms of financial well-being, moral and ethical righteousness, law-abidement, church attendance, and more. What he found and described in Cass County was more than provable prosperity, it was an equal adherence to traditional American ideals. The black pioneers were not just succeeding in reaching their own goals; they were succeeding in reaching and propagating the sacred American dream right down to the picket fence.

"Many of the houses were large, attractive, and well built. The yards were made beautiful with grass, shrubbery, and flowers… We saw little to indicate we were in a negro town except the colors of the faces of the people."

But then, Washington wasn't done yet. It was one thing to prove that the African Americans of Cass County were personally successful and personally righteous and personally accountable. It was another to show their commitment to civic responsibility and to the well-being of all people. For his skeptical audience, it wasn't enough to demonstrate that African Americans could do well for themselves. The bar was even higher.

Washington was left the impossible burden of proving that the freedom of African Americans would provide a greater level of well-being for the white people around them.

It was a difficult argument, but once again, Washington struck gold in Calvin Township; pointing out the tax burdens paid out by wealthy African American landowners, businessmen, and agriculturalists throughout the county.

Washington appears to have been most impressed with a man named Samuel Hawkes, an African-American landowner, moneylender, agriculturalist, and real estate trader. Hawkes was notable as the single largest taxpayer in Calvin Township, owned about five hundred acres of land, and was worth at least $50,000. Adjusting for more than a century of inflation, Hawkes was a self-made and first-generation millionaire.

Successful African Americans in Calvin Township kept their history in poetic and tangible ways. During his visits, Washington noticed fine and stately homes with seven or eight rooms, testaments to the success of the hardworking people who'd toiled and saved to get there. But then behind those homes, Washington often saw something just as important – the roughshod cabins the hardy pioneers built when they first arrived.

The shabby cabins that Washington saw were not the ancient relics or forgotten echoes of a distant past. In the cases of the most prosperous African American families, it was an architectural history that spanned not more than three generations. I want to call all of it incredible, but Booker T. Washington has a different take, and a more correct one at that:

"In the story of this development, there is nothing startling or remarkable. It is simply the story of the growth of a people when given the American chance to grow naturally and gradually."

Unfortunately, it wouldn't be more than another three generations before the history of Cass County would begin to fade away, and three more after that before the confederate flag would make its way north to fly over a state it never represented, in a county that had won victory over its ideals, and above homes built by people who had already proved the thing wrong.

116

CHAPTER NINE

THE TERRIBLE SLAUGHTER ON THE MICHIGAN SOUTHERN RAILROAD

To the modern explorer, the corner of Lincoln Way and Ironwood might feel like an unlikely home to Playland Park, once a regional destination, a thriving amusement park, and host to the biggest parties in South Bend. But for the earliest South Benders, it was an unlikely home for an altogether different reason. That's because, before Playland was home to the Jack Rabbit and the racetrack and the Duke Ellington concert and Babe Ruth's mammoth home run, it was the site of one of South Bend's greatest tragedies.

It was a disaster that started with mismanagement of the region's waterways all the way back in the 1850s, the loudest (but not nearly the last) failure that would define St. Joseph County's relationship with its wetlands and natural resources. Among the other artifacts of a long-expired past, there used to be a rivulet here known as Denslow Creek, a seasonal waterway that flowed from the south and into the St. Joseph River, draining local farmlands in the aftermath of heavy rains. There's not much of an echo of the remains of the ditch, although the stream may have once helped carve the southwesterly route of Twyckenham Drive south of Ewing Street.

Either way, Denslow Creek was significant enough that the Michigan Southern Railroad required a bridge to cross the thing and erected the Springbrook Bridge that would later give Springbrook Park its name. It wasn't nearly the last bridge that would be built to span the waterway.

The hills that rise alongside the southsides of South Bend and Mishawaka present about as much elevation as you get in this part of the country, and while it's not exactly a mountainscape, it is an area that can present significant problems for water managers. During dry spells, Denslow Creek was known to dry hard; but when the rainwater rushed down from the hills, it could inundate the narrow creek:

As usual during a heavy rain the water came down from the big hills south of the railroad track in a seething, boiling, foaming torrent, through the bed of the creek, which at other times is but a dry, sandy waste.

Newspaper accounts are filled with warnings about the creek and are dotted with stories of drownings and capsized boats in the aftermath of even the lightest rains. It seems that people were prone to underestimate the exponential power of the overwhelmed rivulet, and that includes the city engineers. Rather than doing anything to alleviate the seasonal strain on the troublesome waterway, they continued to throw good money after bad, erecting a series of failing bridges that failed to elicit the confidence of the people who knew better.

Farmers and locals had spent years and decades warning local governments that Denslow Creek was inadequate, but water management was difficult and political, infringing on properties and freedoms. Building bridges was much easier, at least in theory.

By 1884, after several attempts at less robust bridges had failed, South Bend made plans to build an unsinkable version. They promised engineering overkill, including 800 feet of mason-grade stonework to span the 20-foot ditch. It would take that kind

118

of assurance to win over a skeptical public, but in September of that same year, the bridge was opened to pedestrians, street cars, and the occasional one-horse open sleigh.[10] The city was sure this bridge would last, but they were wrong.

Nearly two years to the day after the unsinkable Springbrook Bridge was opened, South Bend experienced what the papers called the heaviest rainfall in the history of the city. Several showers dumped on the region throughout the day, including a good-sized hailstorm. But it wasn't until after 8:00 p.m. that the floodgates of heaven fully opened, soaking the city in a downpour that lasted nearly four hours. As the Tribune so poetically put it:

Jupiter Pluvius Puked

The newspaper's account of the storm is terrific, noting that electric lights throughout the city were extinguished by the storm, that frightened pedestrians stumbled into crosswalk gutters, and that horses froze in fear thanks to the tremendous flashes of lightning, making the blackness even darker by contrast. Shingles were torn from houses, livestock were killed, buggies were overturned, and crops were ruined across the county. Hailstones the size of hen's eggs were said to shuck corn cobs clean from the stalk. Some 15,000 panes of glass were shattered at the Oliver Chilled Plow Works.

And of course, the Springbrook Bridge was washed away, "as if it were built of straws". The wreckage was swept down the creek toward the river, and damage was estimated well into the thousands of dollars. A greater tragedy was narrowly avoided when

---

[10] In February 1888, The Tribune reported on a very literal "one horse open sleigh" accident at the Springbrook Bridge that left a pair of Mishawakans injured after their vehicle came into contact with a streetcar line.

a pair of South Benders – Chris Reasor and John Geyer – ventured out into the storm to place obstructions ahead of the wreckage and to warn travelers away from their attempts to cross the thing. And still, it wasn't close to being the worst tragedy in the history of the Springbrook Bridge.

Some 25 years before the unsinkable bridge was swallowed by the hungry creek, there was another bridge. This one was even less impressive and less robust, planted by the Michigan Southern Railroad to navigate its cars and passengers safely across Denslow Creek along its regular route between Chicago and Toledo. Local farmers had warned the railroad about the unpredictability of the rivulet the bridge was designed to span, but the engineers were deaf to their warnings. The railroad company knew their bridge wasn't equipped to deal with heavy flooding, but they were quick to point out that Denslow Creek hadn't flooded in *almost* 20 years! It was a curious defense at best.

Later, it would be the only defense they had.

* * *

The weather came through the same way the weather always does in the Midwest: unpredictably. It was June of 1859, still two years away from the start of the Civil War, and Denslow Creek was about to rage out of control, not for the first time and certainly not for the last. The Studebaker company was less than a decade old, James Oliver had just received his first patent for the chilled plow, and Schuyler Colfax was a 35-year-old serving a term in the Indiana statehouse. The population of a young South Bend was not yet 4,000, but the city was about to make the front page of the New York Times.

It wouldn't be for any of the right reasons.

The official investigation would point to a blocked culvert as the cause of the accident that was about to come, a convenient excuse that would later exculpate the Michigan Southern Railroad of liability. The truth was more sordid and came with more culpability – the railroad had constructed a bridge that was woefully unable to contend with a stream that was historically and knowably prone to flooding.

It was a few minutes before midnight and the Night Express was chugging along from Toledo to Chicago. All day long water had spilled from the skies and then rushed from the hills toward Denslow Creek. Unlike the weather that would come in 1888, this rainfall was not historic nor was it Biblical. But it was steady, and it was enough.

The railroad version of the Springbrook Bridge was weakening by the minute as the weight of the water pressed against it, trying to pull its foundations with it into the St. Joseph River. The bridge strained mightily the same way its builders had designed it to. But all it would take would be a little more weight or perhaps just a little bit of shaking to make the whole thing go.

Unfortunately for the passenger train approaching the compromised bridge, it carried quite a bit of weight and was prone to shaking. In an instant the embankment gave way and the bridge crumbled. The train failed to make the jump across the ravine on its own and plunged headlong into the raging waters of the angry creek. By the time it was over, the scene was a catastrophe.

The engine was literally buried in the opposite side of the ravine in quicksand and mud, and the tender, baggage and express car, and two second class cars, were shattered almost into kindling wood, and piled on the top of the engine.

Early reports pegged the death count as high as 75, accounting for half of the train's capacity, and the South Bend Train Wreck[11] was recorded as the deadliest railway disaster in the history of the United States at the time. The scene was a nightmare, with eyewitnesses reporting a horrifying blend of confusion, screaming, and darkness; punctuated by streaks of lightning across a vindictive sky. Nearly all of the dead were killed by drowning, and several were never fully identified or accounted for. Upon hearing the alarm, citizens rushed to the aid of their fellow man, but in almost every instance, their effort was too late. Families and individuals were swept into the raging waters in

---

[11] In some places, the incident is referred to as the Mishawaka Train Wreck because the wreck happened right at the line between the two cities.

varying states of consciousness, the broken limbs they sustained in the violent collision not injury enough to kill them, at least not yet. A middle-aged woman was buried up to her neck in quicksand. A young boy had been decapitated.

One woman who was with her husband and five children, ran wildly about all night seeking her family, but without success, until morning, when she found them all dead. She then went to a farmhouse a few yards off, where after sitting some minutes, the wretched wife and mother expired.

Newspapers all over the country reported on the tragedy, noting the names of the dead and seeking to explain why the incident had happened as well as why it could never happen in their own communities.

Nearby homes and hotels were turned into makeshift hospitals and recovery rooms for the lucky survivors. The less lucky were identified and buried. The least lucky were mutilated beyond identification and buried in a mass grave at the Mishawaka City Cemetery. A final body count was never established.

Legends and anecdotes tell that the wreckage of the train was never fully removed from the earth, that erosion may have later pulled parts of the locomotive further into the river or that overgrowth may have swallowed it into the land. It's an open question if all of the dead were recovered, or if they were instead swept downstream by the quickening river or buried in the banks of the rivulet along with their steam-powered chariot. In the following decades, farmers tilling their fields along Denslow Creek reported finding remains of bodies and locomotive wreckage, including a fully preserved human rib in 1883.

In the aftermath of America's greatest railway tragedy, the Michigan Southern built a new bridge and engaged in marketing and advertising efforts designed to bolster public confidence in its railways. In fact, it took protests and political action from South Benders and Mishawakans to halt construction of the new bridge long enough to recover the bodies that were known to be buried in the embankment.

Even this effort was not enough. The Michigan Southern was an important line and construction on a new bridge began a few weeks later. After all, the greatest tragedy of the crash would have been the slowing of capitalism. Even the newspapers went out of their way to recount the "good news" from the disaster – that a safe containing more than $60,000 had been recovered along with all of the money that had been inside of it.

During the next decades, the exploits of the occasionally raging creek would become a fixture in the newspapers. Bridges were washed away at the site in 1873, 1875, 1878, 1881, 1886, and 1906. Boating accidents and drownings were common, and at one point in time, armed bandits would rob travelers attempting to cross the bridge in the rain, knowing that authorities would be too fearful to chase them around the volatile stream.

When Springbrook and Playland Parks opened near the spot where Denslow Creek drained into the St. Joseph, it was at the location that was the most historically and statistically dangerous place in South Bend. They even built a roller coaster a stone's throw from the site of what had once been the nation's deadliest rail disaster.

Fortunately for the people running the parks, the city finally conceded to common sense water management in 1906; after the failures of six bridges, dozens of deaths, and a series of crippling financial damages. Denslow Creek was rerouted and replaced. The foaming and ravenous waters that used to rush down from the hills have been tamed, even if the weather was not. The Terrible Slaughter on the Michigan Southern remains the deadliest disaster in the history of St. Joseph County.

DREADFUL RAILROAD SLAUGHTER.

Smash of a Train on the Michigan Southern Road.

Thirty-three Dead Bodies Taken from the Ruins.

FIFTY OR SIX Y WOUNDED.

CLEVELAND, Tuesday, June 28.

A train on the Michigan Southern Railroad was thrown from the track, last nigh', by the washing away of a culvert, and twenty or thirty persons are reported to have been killed. Particulars will be obtained as soon as possible.

CHICAGO, Tuesday, June 28—P. M.

The accident on the Michigan Southern Railroad, last night, occurred near South Bend, Indiana. The stream, where it took place, is naturally a small rivulet, but was much swollen by heavy rains the previous afternoon and evening, and the flood of wood which passed down, probably checked the culvert converting the embankment into a dam, and the great weight of water, with the concussion of the crossing train, caused the sad calamity.

125

CHAPTER TEN
CROOKED CARDS AND
STRAIGHT WHISKEY

Fewer than a hundred years after a handful of brave African American pioneers proved that they were more than capable of achieving the American dream if only given half-a-chance, a group of counter-culturalists would emerge from San Francisco's bohemian underbelly to let the world know that the American dream was never worth chasing to begin with. Led by literary giants like John Kerouac and Allen Ginsberg, the Beats challenged the very notions that Americans had been taught and instructed to strive toward for generations.

Of course, throughout the history of the United States, there had always been anarchists, pacifists, hedonists, artists, organic pharmaceutical experimenters, counter-culturalists, and anti-culturalists. But the Beat writers liberated those kinds of dangerous views from the hovels, dark alleys, and asylums where they had usually been stashed away, so as not corrupt the perfectly Puritanically ambitious American public.

But thanks to Kerouac and Ginsberg, and along with peers like Gary Snyder, Gregory Corso, and Lawrence Ferlinghetti; counter-culturalism crept into the forefront of the American psyche during the 1950s, mutating the DNA of a nation looking for its identity in a postwar world. The same blue jeans that had once been relegated to the laborers in the mines became the uniform of a generation. The Beats created a movement that would change the fabric of America forever, and like all movements, it was the kind of thing that needed to start somewhere.

It started in South Bend.

A newish historical marker at 828 Park Avenue remembers that an important man was born there, once upon a time at a nearby hospital in South Bend, although even that was very nearly not the case, at least according to the man's own (mostly fictional) autobiography. According to his own pen, the man's mother was in Elkhart when she began to experience the pains of labor. They'd planned on going to a hospital in Chicago for the birth and loaded themselves onto a train for that very reason, but the woman's child was eager to make his appearance so that he could begin to change the world. By the time the train blew its whistle in South Bend, the time had come. The woman and her husband rushed off of the thing and made their way to the hospital.

And that's how Kenneth Rexroth came to be born in South Bend, the son of a traveling pharmaceutical salesman named Charles. The birth hadn't been easy, and as it would turn out, the boy's life wasn't going to prove to be any easier. In fact, his days at the Park Avenue home were just about as good as his childhood was going to get.

It was on Park Avenue that little Kenneth learned to read at a young age and was exposed to the earliest parts of his mother's well-curated classical education. She read to him classical mythologies and exposed him to science and world history lessons at an age when most children were learning the alphabet. Throughout his life, Kenneth was especially fascinated by the history of the Indians and their connection to the earth. As a child, he would come to befriend and admire a local Indian herb farmer who was rumored to be more than 90 years old. All of these experiences would help feed the man that Kenneth Rexroth would become, but there was perhaps another more seminal experience that would solidify it.

It was just a few years on Park Avenue before it was time for the Rexroths to move along again. By the time Kenneth was four, the family had moved onto Beardsley Avenue in Elkhart, into another prestigious home in an elite neighborhood on a proud street. The family had worked hard, earned money, and gained status. They had realized their American Dream. It should have been the moment when everything was coming together. Instead, it was the moment when everything started to fall apart.

The two years he spent in their Beardsley Avenue home must have been formative for the young Kenneth Rexroth. He had seen his parents achieve everything that good Americans were supposed to aspire toward, and just as much, he had seen that it did not make them happy.

All of their successes could not keep Kenneth's parents from falling further into alcoholism, chronic illness, and gambling addiction. By the time he turned 11, Kenneth was essentially orphaned. His mother had died of tuberculosis and his father was in and out of sanitariums for his drinking problem. As Rexroth would later write of his father in *Proust's Madeleine*:

I can hear him coming home drunk
From the Elks' Club in Elkhart
Indiana, bumping the
Chairs in the dark. I can see
Him dying of cirrhosis
Of the liver and stomach
Ulcers and pneumonia,
Or, as he said on his deathbed, of
Crooked cards and straight whiskey,
Slow horses and fast women.

After the loss of his father, death of his mother, and even the death of his Indian mentor, Rexroth was left to the streets, first in Toledo and then in Chicago. The teenage Kenneth Rexroth was a troublemaker and a hustler, committing low-level crimes and working as an errand boy for lewd and semi-legal business endeavors including gambling houses and burlesque clubs.

Rexroth had an incredible knack for being in certain places during consequential moments. When he unwittingly became part of the Toledo Labor Riots, it steeled his young mind as a labor sympathizer and an enemy of the capitalist agenda.

By the time he was ready for the ninth grade, thanks to his mother's influence, Rexroth was better read than any of his peers. And thanks to his divergent life experiences, he was more willing to question the wisdom of the mythology of The American Way. In short, he wasn't the kind of student built to succeed in an American high school in 1920. It was a world where divergent views were neither welcome nor rewarded. Rexroth was a free-thinker and an establishment-questioner who also happened to be intelligent enough and articulate enough to espouse his views among his yet-uncorrupted high school peers.

He was expelled almost immediately.

Left to discover his own education, a sixteen-year-old Kenneth Rexroth pulled off his most impressive trick to date. Somehow, the orphaned, troublemaking, high school dropout infiltrated the highest order thought salons in Chicago and found himself regularly exchanging ideas with the likes of Carl Sandburg, D.H. Lawrence, Eugene Debs, and Frank Lloyd Wright:

I went there night after night and sat quietly in the corner and left long after midnight to travel back to the South Side in the cold empty rattling elevated trains, my head full of fireworks. Every time I heard a book mentioned I wrote it down and went to the library and got it out and read it. Every time I heard a subject discussed that I didn't understand I did my best to bone up on it.

It wasn't long into this education when Rexroth's disparate life experiences collided with his first taste of steady employment. As a soapboxer for the IWW, Rexroth memorized and recited labor poems, excerpts from Upton Sinclair, and the occasional sanitized socialist manifesto. Rexroth was good at it, and during his performances, the gathered crowds were persuaded to sign up for their own union cards. The unionization strategy worked well enough that eventually the IWW paid Rexroth to take his show on the road, but when my dad was a union steward in the 90s, I don't think he ever read one poem to the other Teamsters ever.

131

In between his itinerant soapboxing gigs, Rexroth taught himself to paint and managed to keep up his self-education, joining a collection of humanity that called itself the Washington Park Bug Club. He described the group as the kind of idea exchange unheard of since the time of ancient Greece:

Here, every night until midnight could be heard passionate exponents of every variety of human lunacy. There were Anarchist-Single-Taxers, British-Israelites, self-anointed archbishops of the American Catholic Church, Druids, Anthroposophists, mad geologists who had proven the world was flat or that the surface of the earth was the inside of a hollow sphere, and people who were in communication with the inhabitants of Mars, Atlantis, and Tibet, severally and sometimes simultaneously.

By 21, Kenneth Rexroth had already lived several lives. He'd invested in a jazz club, worked a brief stint as a newspaper reporter on the divorce court beat, spent a year in prison, married the artist Andrée Schafer, and was preparing for a road trip to California, where, whether he knew it or not, he was about to start a fire that would never stop burning.

*   *   *

Kenneth and Andrée Rexroth hitched their way across the United States, landing in San Francisco with no money and no plan. They both took jobs painting furniture and poured their free time into one another and their varied pursuits – art, writing, and exploring the outdoors. Rexroth's early writing is critical of the developers and capitalists who seemed intent on destroying the beauty and sanctity of the earth, making him one of the earliest American environmental writers.

But Rexroth would not come to be known as the father of the environmental poetry movement. He was an early pacifistic poet, but he would not come to be known as the father of that movement either. He was among the earliest western adopters of eastern philosophies, including Buddhism and yoga; but this would also not become his legacy.

Seeking to replicate the salons that he had experienced in Chicago, Rexroth began to cultivate his own literary coterie in San Francisco; inviting poets, artists, and other interesting freethinkers to gatherings at his home. Conversations typically turned toward poetry, politics, and jazz; and indeed, Rexroth's work tended to blend all three. He even released two albums in the 50s of his own poetry readings while the Dave Brubeck Quartet played alongside. Pioneering the idea of reading poetry over music has even led some to call Kenneth Rexroth the first rapper, although that distinction certainly does not appear on the historical marker in front of his old South Bend home.

It was during one of these performances that Rexroth trotted out a brand new poet he'd met during the salon gatherings at his own home. The poet's name was Allen Ginsberg, and the poem he shared was "Howl". The Beat Movement was officially off the ground and running. It was never going to look back.

For his part, Rexroth was a reluctant father to the movement. He was incredibly generous to and supportive of the earliest poets of the Beat Generation, but watched with disappointment as the movement went off the rails, at least in his own view. He decried the way that the literary movement he started devolved into a trend. He derided Kerouac and others for what he saw as the shameful seeking of commercial success.

For Rexroth, the later Beats were sellouts, peddling their own rejection of the American Dream in order to make enough money to achieve it. He didn't need to look any further than the blue jean pant to prove his case. Once a symbol of the anarchist rebellion, they'd become part of the standard uniform of a standard America by the late fifties. The Beats had once pushed back against the American Dream; but at some point, they had managed to become only a variation of the thing. By 1958, Rexroth dismissed the Beat movement as "a publicity gimmick in the hands of Madison Avenue" that would fade away soon enough. He was wrong. Seventy years later, we're still waiting for blue jeans to go out of style, and the echoes of the Beats have not been silenced by the unceasing march of culture and time.

It's not an exaggeration. It wasn't just Ginsberg and Kerouac that Rexroth launched into the mainstream. It was Bob Dylan too; and as I write this paragraph, Dylan is playing to a sold-out crowd in Seville, Spain. The Beats aren't going anywhere, and for all of his criticism of what the Beat movement had become, Rexroth never stopped being a fan of Bob Dylan, although he probably never expected that the singer would become his most enduring creation. In 1966, Rexroth acknowledged that:

Dylan is probably the most important event to happen in recent poetry, and he's created the American beginning of a tradition as old as civilization in France.

So maybe Rexroth did eventually make peace with the Beat movement he'd helped to launch. Either way, he found he could not stop or stall what the thing had become, nor would he be able to escape his role in creating it. Although he outlived many of the Beat writers who'd become most synonymous with their generational angst, and even though he experienced a long and distinguished second career as a literary professor, writer, and critic; Rexroth would always be associated with his role in launching the Beat Generation. Upon his death in 1982, the obituary in the *New York Times* ran a headline calling him a "Father Figure to Beat Poets."

Of course, Kenneth Rexroth wasn't around to dispute the claims of his own obituary, and maybe he wouldn't have seen the need. After all, if he wasn't the beginning of the movement, he was its prelude; an undeniable influence on the movement that would change the fabric of American culture forever.

In 1973, at the age of 68, Kenneth Rexroth returned to South Bend for a literary festival at Notre Dame. He spent the night at the home of English professor John Matthias, one of the adorable houses on Lafayette Boulevard near Leeper Park. Later that night, as the conversation wound down, Rexroth wandered into the cool night to see if he could track down his childhood home, just a half-a-block away. He couldn't do it.

Of course, there wasn't a historical marker in front of the home then. It would be more than forty years before there would be. If Kenneth Rexroth had forgotten his place in South Bend, it is fair to say that South Bend had forgotten him too.

In my childhood when I first
Saw myself unfolded in
The triple mirrors, in my
Youth, when I pursued myself
Wandering roads like a roving
Masterless dog, when I met
Myself on sharp peaks of ice,
And tasted myself dissolved
In the lulling heavy sea,
In the talking night, in the
Spiralling stars, what did I know?

CHAPTER ELEVEN

THE BOMBING OF THE PALACE

The year was 1935 and it was a great time to own a newspaper in South Bend. The Tribune and the News-Times blanketed the community with morning and afternoon issues, Sunday specials, and noteworthy extras whenever hard news would hit. Reporters were busy and readers were hungry to catch up on what seemed to be a never-ending supply of unbelievable and sensational stories, with casts of characters more compelling than anything the Hollywood scriptwriters could have come up with. Boys hawked papers on streetcorners, barking headlines that wrote themselves to readers who were desperate to be in the know about the gossip, the crime beat, business scandals, and political drama.

There was the trial of Bruno Hauptmann, charged with the kidnapping and murder of the Lindbergh baby, a story and soap opera that had captivated national attention for nearly three years. A series of trials exposed titillating and sordid details about the recently deceased John Dillinger and the recently incarcerated Al Capone. In more positive news, the nation was gripped by Amelia Earhart's successful attempt to become the first person to fly solo from Hawaii to California. In local sports, Notre Dame was more popular than ever, and South Bend papers offered pages and pages of coverage for every varsity sport the university offered. In baseball, Babe Ruth was limping toward retirement; and of course, there were the Chicago Cubs, 100-game winners and National League champions thanks to an unprecedented 21-game winning streak that saw them through the fall.

But on January 10, it didn't matter what was happening in the rest of the nation. In South Bend, all of those headlines were about to be quite literally blown off the front page altogether.

It was early on the morning of January 10 that the first of three explosions rocked downtown South Bend, emanating from somewhere within the Palais Royale building. The shock of the blasts shook the nearby Hotel LaSalle and tossed hotel guests from their beds. By the time the confused sleepers wandered to their windows to investigate the clatter, they saw the wreckage and the aftermath, another bomb blast and another. A young man sprinted from the scene of the crime and dove into a waiting getaway car, calling out to his co-conspirators:

That was a honey!

The Palace Café took the brunt of the damage as windows shattered and support beams collapsed in the explosion. The establishment was immediately deemed a total loss. The neighboring Dixie Frock Shop was also decimated, and more than a dozen businesses on the surrounding block saw their windows shattered. A nearby jewelry store was an additional casualty of the explosion; doubly so when early morning looters and souvenir-hunters were able to pilfer valuables from the wreckage that had been tossed by the explosion onto downtown sidewalks.

Merchandise from businesses was strewn about Colfax and Michigan Streets, hundreds of feet in every direction. An evening patrolman in neighboring Mishawaka reported hearing the blasts even though he was five miles away. Preliminary estimates put the damage at more than $150,000; more than $3 million in today's money. The wreckage extended into parts of South Bend's public infrastructure, and the hands of a downtown clock stopped moving, freezing in place the time of the South Bend bombing.

It had all gone down at 3:48 a.m. The city was quiet. Besides the bombers, there had not been foot traffic on the streets. Only the night watchman had been in the building, and he was fortunate to have been in the basement when the explosions went off. Either by miracle or by design, there were no casualties and there were no injuries, save for a handful of cats that patrolled the grounds to keep the mice under control.

While shopkeepers and building owners rushed to rebuild and reopen, South Bend police were joined by amateur detectives, insurance inspectors, and investigative journalists trying to get to the bottom of the thing. Authorities had decided quickly that the bombing had been carried out by hired hands, probably out-of-towners with no connection to South Bend, to the Palais Royale, or to the Palace Café.

Gang hideouts in many of the nation's larger cities were being combed for the persons responsible for the bombing after the several experts had consensus of opinion that it was the work of professionals in that line.

South Bend detectives would have a rough go of it looking for pyrotechnicians to out themselves in seedy gangster hovels. It was going to be hard to figure out who detonated the things, but maybe it would be easier to figure out who hired them.

It wouldn't be. In fact, the whole affair would prove to be a difficult investigation and not because they didn't have any suspects.

It was because they had too many.

The night before a series of explosions rocked South Bend, a rowdy group of union musicians were picketing outside the

Palais Royale, one of the few venues in town that hired non-union orchestras. These labor disputes were always contentious and occasionally violent.

The fact that the union musicians had been so visibly present with their vitriol made them an attractive target for the earliest theories of the armchair detectives. Even the Chicago Tribune seized on the union musicians, stating in the immediate aftermath of the decimation that the attack was almost certainly triggered by a labor dispute. Conspiracists were quick to point out that it seemed the professionals had taken care not to damage the attached Palais Royale theater, the place where the musicians stood to lose the most in the case of a closure. In fact, the Palais Royale would reopen almost immediately, hosting the Platinum Blonde revue for a three-day stint just four days after the explosions that rocked the city block.

For reasons that were never made entirely clear, police did little to pursue the unionist theory that had so immediately impacted the press. Probably it's because they'd already become set on a pair of more probable leads, just as salacious, and backed this time with actual evidence. Police made arrests and releases. They captured and interrogated suspects. They conducted dozens of interviews with material and character witnesses. Anonymous tips poured in via telegram and postcard. There were whispers that the federal agents might get involved with the investigation. Just as they were beginning to get their ducks in a row, Police Chief Laurence Lane issued a reassuring promise to the people of South Bend that the case would be solved:

There will be no letup in our investigation, and we are confident the guilty parties will be brought to justice. It is inconceivable that anyone could come into South Bend, blow up one of our buildings, and get away with it.

The musicians weren't their first suspects and they weren't their only suspects either. By the end of the third day of inquiries, police had settled on three new theories worth pursuing; and in the end, it wasn't the ballistics experts or the undercover assets buried deep in the seedy Chicago gang scene who would come up with the clues.

It was the accountants.

A look into the books at the Palais Royale revealed inconsistencies and betrayals, leading detectives to seize the place's financial and business records. James Stasinos, a Greek immigrant and owner of the Palace Café, was held briefly under technical arrest and subjected to questioning in the presence of his lawyers.

Six months before the detonations, Stasinos had an ugly falling out with a pair of business partners, William Zagouras and Christ Kapsimales. Zagouras and Kapsimales felt they were "forced out" of the restaurant and were left to file for bankruptcy as the partnership dissolved. With an established motive for revenge, the two were detained for questioning in the hours just after the bombing, then ultimately released when detectives could provide no evidence against them.

The next week, the Feds were in South Bend, requisitioned on a technicality since the Palais Royale building was run on a federal receivership. Their experts expressed a belief that there had been four bombs instead of three and found evidence of marine-style fuses that were the hallmark of a Chicago bombing outfit.

James Stasinos had deep connections throughout Chicago, where he had once owned a confectionary and where he'd spent the six days leading up to the bombing of his South Bend restaurant. Now, all eyes were on him.

In the good times, the Palace Café had been a popular hangout for college and high school students, especially for those looking to sneak a little bit of liquor to drink in the corner booths. Except for a stint where the place was briefly boycotted by Notre Dame students for kicking out patrons who didn't spend enough money, business looked good from the outside. There were always lots of customers, the place seated to capacity on its busy corner of downtown South Bend.

But an analysis of the Palace Café's accounting revealed that despite its popularity, the place had been hemorrhaging money for years. Stasinos was still making debt service payments on loans he'd taken out during the Depression and was often late paying employees and other debtors. It was no secret within the community or the police investigating the bombing of his restaurant that Stasinos was in a financial dire strait.

So, when they also discovered that Stasinos had taken out two separate insurance policies against the Palace Café and that the most recent policy was designed to explicitly protect his business interests against bomb attacks, Chief Lane became more than a little suspicious. James Stasinos and his wife, Orrie, were arrested on April 7 and charged with conspiracy and insurance fraud.

The Stasinos trial wasn't quite the Lindbergh baby, but in South Bend, it wasn't far off. In January 1936, a parade of more than 100 witnesses came forward to take turns vilifying and exonerating James and Orrie Stasinos. There were allegations of unpaid salaries that helped prove the insolvency of the business. Another witness swore that Stasinos participated in regular shady meetings with shady characters. Chief Lane testified that Stasinos had the countenance and unsurprise of a guilty man when he was informed about the attack on his restaurant.

There was the testimony of a convicted bank robber that put Stasinos at a Chicago restaurant with Danny Kaffee, a known "torch man" with a gang of professional Chicago bombers. There was evidence that Stasinos had another debt in Chicago set to begin repayments just a few days before the bombs went off. There was the testimony of the insurance agent who sold Stasinos his policy, noting that "Mr. Stasinos was very keen to make sure the policy would pay out in the case of a bombing." There was a busted door lock that turned up in the rubble of the explosion, with part of its key still wedged inside, evidence that someone from the inside had been a part of the scheme.

It might have seemed damning, but the Stasinos defense had an answer for every accusation that the prosecution could throw at them. Disgruntled and unpaid employees had as much reason to blow up the Palace Café as Stasinos himself did. Private meetings did not prove any crime. Countenance was not evidence. Convicted bank robbers were wholly unreliable witnesses. Lots of people had debt. The insurance company was vilifying the defendant because they don't want to pay out. The key in question had been lost for some time and possibly stolen. And as for the police? Well, they attached themselves too exclusively too early to the guilt of James Stasinos and failed to adequately investigate the socialist union workers or the shady men that Stasinos had once called his partners.

In the end, the jury was left with at least a reasonable doubt. James and Orrie Stasinos were found not guilty after less than three hours of deliberations, and the ecstatic restaurateur stuck around to personally shake the hands of each juror. He and his wife stepped out to a waiting crowd where Stasinos gave a brief statement and promised he would open another restaurant.

That might have been the end of the story, but its epilogue was filled with even more courtroom drama to be eagerly snatched up by the papers. Stasinos ended up taking his insurers to court to force them to pay out their policies. Once, while being examined by an opposing lawyer, Stasinos came out of his seat in anger when he was asked if he remembered once conspiring to blow the building up himself. When that strategy didn't work, they tried to pin him for exaggerating his losses beyond what was reasonable. None of it worked and eventually the insurance companies were compelled to pay out.

The echoes of the bombing returned in 1939 when Stasinos finally followed through on his plan to open a new downtown South Bend restaurant. His attempts to obtain a liquor license for the Nip-n-Sip were stalled and held up by creditors he'd failed to repay and by those who were still convinced the man was behind the bombing of his own restaurant.

After going silent for a few years, save for a handful of parking tickets, Stasinos would turn up in Pensacola, Florida; where he opened a restaurant called the Romana Bar & Grill and a bar called the Azalea Cocktail Lounge. In 1949, he was arrested on charges involving the illegal sale of liquor. The charges didn't stick. The Azalea Cocktail Lounge remains in business today.

James Stasinos died in Florida in 1964 at the age of 79. The bombing of the Palace Café is still considered unsolved.

CHAPTER TWELVE
THE BULLPEN AT THE SOUTH BEND NEWS-TIMES

For most of the first half of the 20th Century, South Bend was a two-newspaper town. The Tribune and the News-Times fought for scoops and stories and subscribers, each trying to nudge the other a little closer to irrelevancy. Somehow the Tribune came out of the slugfest on top and the News-Times shuttered operations in 1938, unable to fully emerge from the other side of the Great Depression. To be sure, there were financial problems and business issues that the paper couldn't solve; but for all of its failures, the South Bend News-Times would never be able to blame its writers, an unexpectedly impressive group of individuals with deep and wide-reaching plaudits far beyond local news.

The newsroom once included Charles Butterworth a man who would later move onto the New York Times, onto Vaudeville and Broadway, onto the silver screen, and eventually onto the Hollywood Walk of Fame. Butterworth was a bona fide star with more than 30 film credits to his name, including a starring role alongside Clark Gable in *Forsaking All Others*.

Despite his otherwise serious expression, Butterworth's wheelhouse was deadpan comedy. Unlike other actors who freely dealt in over-the-top cheese, Butterworth's delivery was more subtle, occasionally tilting toward the kind of anti-comedy that would still play well today. It was a popular, but sometimes divisive shtick, earning either praise or derision from New York Times columnist Alma Whitaker, who called Butterworth a:

professional silly ass

Butterworth's old cohorts at the News-Times would have likely agreed with the assessment. When the young reporter played a prank on his bosses by fictitiously reporting the death of a prominent South Bend citizen, they fired him from his duties. It's uncertain if the obituary actually ran or if the joke was caught before the paper went to press. Either way, I spent way too long in the microfilm trying to find it.

Butterworth's termination from the News-Times forced him out of South Bend and ended up being just the thing to jumpstart his impressive second career. And even though the Butterworth name doesn't immediately call forth echoes of old Hollywood, his legacy lives on in a truly unexpected way.

Today, despite his undeniable success as a star on the stage and the screen, Butterworth's influence echoes at every grocery store in America. That's because he is literally the inspiration for the beloved naval cereal mascot, Cap'n Crunch.

Of course, Charles Butterworth wasn't the only superstar to pass through the News-Times on his way to bigger and better things. After all, this was the same newsroom that once featured a young Ring Lardner before he would reinvent sports coverage, humor, and political commentary for generations to come.

With a parade of future stars passing through the doors of the News-Times and into its rotating bullpen, it would seem to be an impossible task to hire new writers to replace the old ones. After all, how do you replace a Ring Lardner when he is ready to be launched to greener pastures?

But if the News-Times had anything, it had a nose for finding talented writers. Remember, even Lardner had been an accidental hire who talked his way into the position with embellishments, exaggerations, and the occasional outright lie.

By the time Lardner made his move to Chicago, the News-Times already had a succession plan in place, another writer waiting in the wings. Lardner's assistant, J.P. McEvoy, would be tasked with taking the sports beat.

There were going to be big shoes to fill.

McEvoy was ready to fill them.

*   *   *

The first miracle of J.P. McEvoy's young life was that he ever made it to South Bend in the first place. It's kind of a mystery how he arrived when and where he did, but then most of McEvoy's early life is kind of a mystery.

There were questions about his birthplace and his birthday; even questions about his birthyear. Orphaned at a young age, McEvoy would go on to recount that he was "probably" born in New York City between 1894 and 1897. Adoption took McEvoy to the tiny town of New Burnside in southern Illinois where he became son to an Irish immigrant who'd once been a mathematical astronomer at the University of Dublin. What work there was for him in New Burnside is another one of the unanswered mysteries surrounding McEvoy's childhood. Writing in the third person, McEvoy recounted that he:

...doesn't remember where he was born—but has been told that it was New York City and that the year was 1894. He doesn't know whether this was a good year to be born in or not, and is glad now that nothing can be done about it. He didn't go to school—he was dragged. This went on for a number of years, during which time McEvoy grew stronger and stronger—until finally he couldn't be dragged any more. This was officially called the end of his education...

Except it wasn't the end of the boy's education. Not even close. In 1910, when he was either 16 or 13 but probably closer to 16, McEvoy enrolled at the University of Notre Dame and prepared to hustle and grind his way toward a college degree. He attended classes and worked as an on-campus waiter, but discovered he needed a second job to cover tuition. That's how he came to be hired as a cub sports reporter at the News-Times. For the remainder of his college career, McEvoy would earn his tuition payments by taking on the second-string sporting assignments behind the paper's blossoming star, Ring Lardner.

The writing seemed to come easy for J.P. McEvoy, but sports did not. His first assignment was to cover a local baseball game, and McEvoy became so preoccupied with wordsmithing the descriptions of the action on the field that he forgot to record or recall the score of the game, nor make mention of who won the thing. But there was a glimmer of something impressive in the boy's writing and the News-Times invested in developing the talent they saw in him.

Incredibly, the New York orphan with a gift for words had landed in the one place best suited to nurture his unique gifts. His adopted parents had been Irish academics who passed along a set of values (and a surname) that would point their son toward the University of Notre Dame. And then, every night after class, McEvoy would sit beneath the tutelage of Ring Lardner, developing his voice, his humor, and his understanding of the contests he was sent to cover. Given all that, maybe McEvoy's next success shouldn't have come as such a surprise to those who'd followed his story.

*   *   *

John Striebel was not a unique newspaper boy under the employ of Edgar Stoll and the South Bend News-Times. He spent his days running papers to diners and drugstores in exchange for a couple of nickels and earned a few extra pennies when he'd hawk papers on the street corners. At the end of the shift or when the newspapers ran out, Striebel would spend a tiny portion of his earnings on a soda, before returning to the News-Times bullpen to talk baseball with the other boys.

Once, during a particularly boring day, Striebel deigned to entertain the squad by drawing a caricature of the circulation manager on a newly whitewashed basement wall. It didn't take long before Striebel's handiwork was discovered and not much longer after that before one of his cohorts ratted the artist out.

155

John Striebel was summoned straightaway to the editor's office. He came for a scolding he knew he deserved and apologized profusely preemptively for mocking his boss.

Edgar Stoll wouldn't hear it.

In 1905, at the same time he was taking a chance on Ring Lardner, Stoll was making another non-traditional hire, bringing on board a 14-year-old newspaper boy as his lead political cartoonist, based entirely on a piece of basement graffiti that was never supposed to be discovered. In the blink of an eye, John Striebel had been transformed from a newspaper boy into the youngest political commentator in the nation.

The former newspaper boy was well-respected during his early career at the News-Times, and he remained accountable to his superiors and his deadlines. Despite his lack of formal art training, his style was not crude. Despite his age, his commentary was shrewd and insightful. Despite his experience, his countenance was professional and impressive.

Striebel was even known to jump in and cover actual news stories as a reporter when the paper was shorthanded. Besides all of that, the boy was as strict in his personal affairs as he was at work, saving his pay so that he could attend college at Notre Dame. He maintained his work at the News-Times throughout his schooling and became fast friends with a classmate and coworker named J.P. McEvoy.

Striebel's career took him to a Chicago advertising firm and then to the Chicago Tribune where he penned popular comic strips, including *Pantomime*, which was syndicated in newspapers throughout the country. The strip was received favorably, with one reviewer saying:

It combines in one the best elements of the modern strip, the sketch from life, and the daily cartoon, with all the humor and all the punch of the best comics, without being the least low-brow. It is a refreshingly radical departure from the well worn paths of comic art. Striebel ranks today as one of the most widely known and highly paid artists in the Mid West.

Although his early comics earned critical and popular acclaim, Striebel wanted more. In particular, he wanted more legitimacy as an artist, so in 1924, he and his wife moved to New York where Striebel studied painting, produced fine art, and began painting magazine covers. Striebel's star was bright, but the best was yet to come.

Meanwhile, J.P. McEvoy was completing his education and graduating beyond the pages of the News-Times. His next stop was the Chicago Tribune where he worked as a sportswriter and authored comic strips for the papers. He created a handful of limited-run serials and even spent some time writing *Charlie Chaplin's Comic Capers*, a strip that is absolutely everything you expect it to be. In this one, a man beats a dog with a wooden stool in a case of mistaken identity, and that's it. That's the punchline.

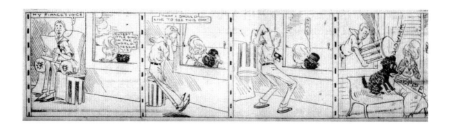

Besides his comics and his work for the paper, he also worked as editor for a company that specialized in publishing postcards and greeting cards. The company even published a pair of McEvoy's earliest books, including <u>The Sweet Dry and Dry, Or, See America Thirst!</u>, a book of observations about Prohibition.

They tell me this here prohibish'
Is good for fowl and flesh and fish,
That countless blessing ooze and flow
From flirting with the H 2 0,
And highballs made of rain and dew
Are very good for me and you...
Well, mebbe so, I dunno.

McEvoy made waves as a Chicago creative. He entertained national interviews and regional audiences and befriended luminaries like Frank Lloyd Wright. He was even known to turn up at the same salons and parlors that were frequented by Kenneth Rexroth, a man he'd once lived just a few blocks away from during his time in South Bend.

During his time in Chicago, McEvoy collaborated just once with his old friend, John Striebel. The two worked together on a full-page weekly serial called *The Potters* that would be syndicated throughout the United States. With the success of the serial, New York became aware of J.P. McEvoy, and it wouldn't be long before the man made his next move.

McEvoy moved to Manhattan and became an immediate hit in the city. *The Potters* had been adapted to a stage play, and the play was a success. The New York Times, desperate to include McEvoy on its roster, offered a columnist spot with no strings attached. McEvoy could write whatever he wanted as often as he wanted. The Times just wanted to be in the business of J.P. McEvoy. It would prove to be a good investment.

During his first years at the Times, *The Potters* was published as a book and McEvoy was the author of a popular autobiographical column at the paper. He contributed to *The Ziegfeld Follies of 1925* alongside Will Rogers and W.C. Fields.

In 1928, now both New Yorkers, McEvoy and Striebel would collaborate on another serial, *Show Girl in Hollywood*, a story about an aspiring Hollywood actress named Dixie Dugan. *Show Girl* would go on to become a novel and stage play before it became a pair of Hollywood films starring Alice White.

By the middle part of the 1920s, J.P. McEvoy was a bankable quantity in journalism in Chicago and New York, a nationally syndicated comic and serial writer, a several-times published novelist, a regular figure in Broadway writing rooms, and a coveted contributor to Hollywood films. The New York Times recognized the star they had on their hands and wanted to do whatever they could to keep him on the payroll. They offered him a personal assistant to help manage his schedule, keep his notes, and sort his correspondence.

Maybe McEvoy recognized the man who showed up for the interview. Maybe they bonded over the fact that they had both once worked for Edgar Stoll at the South Bend News-Times. Either way, McEvoy offered the job to the man on the other side of his desk. It had been a long road for both of them to get there, but now Charles Butterworth had a job as J.P. McEvoy's secretary at the New York Times.

*   *   *

McEvoy had been working for a long time on a new kind of project, almost as if he had a drive to invest himself into every medium of performance art that existed. This one was a humorous musical revue, a song and dance show featuring McEvoy's lyrics in songs like "American Revue Girls", "Riverside Bus", and "Tabloid Papers."

He called the show *Americana*.

Americana was McEvoy's first foray into music, but it was far from a second-rate production. It opened at the Belmont Theatre, starred Lew Brice and Roy Atwell, and included music by none other than George Gershwin. It was a scatterbrained collection of seemingly unrelated vignettes including an absurd jazz opera, a scathing satire of tabloid newspapers, a good-natured mockery of American folk songs, a burlesque Hamlet, and a parody of Rotary Clubs.

Most reviewers concluded that the Rotary bit was the strongest of the group. In that number, the speaker is tasked with introducing the newest members of the group, including the "crutch tipper", who puts rubber tips on crutches, the "bear optician", whose job is to place the glass eyes into bear rugs, and the "meat costumer" whose principal task is to "put the panties on the lamb chops".

McEvoy spent much of his time at the New York Times cleaning up the silly lyrics to his silly songs and running them past his new secretary for a second opinion, the two laughing uproariously at each other in the bullpen at The New York Times. Butterworth contributed much of the material for the Rotary sketch, and it didn't take much pleading from Butterworth before McEvoy allowed him an audition.

Butterworth didn't miss his opportunity.

He nailed the audition and landed a small role in the revue. His deadpan delivery was unique, but only served to elevate the ridiculousness of the source material around him. Every experienced actor on the set agreed that only Butterworth would be allowed to deliver the Rotary speech, and from that point on, the deadpan actor from South Bend would be a career actor.

Another News-Times alum had become a star.

Time Magazine remarked that Butterworth, then "utterly unknown to Broadway" was the funniest performer. A review in New York World could not recall such an "inexperienced player making such an impression". In a show filled with stars, Charles Butterworth had stolen the spotlight from all of them. He wouldn't need to beg his hometown acquaintances to let him audition for their shows any longer. Based on his success in *Americana*, studios and theaters would be begging Butterworth to appear in their shows. During the next 20 years, his newfound fame would lead him into deep and lasting friendships with dignitaries like Oscar Hammerstein and Fred Astaire.

*   *   *

As for Striebel and McEvoy, they were busy collaborating on a new project that would become their most lasting legacy.

They'd decided to revive the character of Dixie Dugan, pulling her from their serials, novels, and movies in order to reinvent her as a daily comic strip character. Striebel and McEvoy imagined following Dugan's trials and tribulations as an aspiring actress but were forced to pivot when the stock market crashed a week after the first strip ran, plunging Americans into the Great Depression.

All of a sudden, a spoiled aspiring starlet didn't seem like the kind of relatable and sympathetic character that Americans wanted or needed. McEvoy made the call to switch things up, and for the rest of her run, Dixie Dugan would play the role of a former actress working odd jobs to get by. She spent a stint as a secretary, another as a schoolteacher, and five years as a stewardess. Along the way, she entertained many potential suitors, although none of them worked out in the end.

While the tone of the strip began as a lighthearted comedy, it spent long periods existing as something like a soap opera, albeit a soap opera about a woman that was very obviously written by a group of men. Dixie's on-and-off romances and love triangles delivered interest even when they didn't deliver laughs. A significant storyline followed Dixie's brother when he experienced facial injuries while fighting overseas, so much so that he was rendered unrecognizable. During these drawn-out story arcs, the strip would occasionally go days or even weeks without making a joke or reaching for a laugh. In this way and in many others, *Dixie Dugan* was a pioneer in a world where comic strips usually existed for short runs and were designed to elicit cheap gags.

The endeavor would become a family affair for the McEvoys and Striebels. Eventually, McEvoy turned the writing over to his son, Denny. And true to form, Striebel's daughter Margaret was hired to handle the strip's lettering at the ripe age of 14. The *Dixie Dugan* comic strip would inspire another film adaptation in 1943, but this version would prove to be a flop and planned sequels were scrapped.

J.P. McEvoy's star would remain bright, although he became more selective and less prodigious with his work during the second half of his career. McEvoy was tapped to write the Shirley Temple film, *Just Around the Corner.*

It's uncertain if Lardner, Butterworth, McEvoy, or Striebel maintained sentimentality for the city of South Bend, if they ever returned to visit their old stomping grounds, or if they ever checked in on the bullpen at the newspaper where each of them had been given their start. The four superstars from the South Bend News-Times had each made their mark on journalism, culture, and publishing. They'd each become movers and shakers on screen, on stage, and in culture; and many of their creations would last beyond their own earthly lives.

Lardner died in New York in 1933, but his son Ring Lardner, Jr. was well on his way to a career as a Hollywood screenwriter, where he would win two Academy Awards[12] and become the face of the "Hollywood Ten" when he was blacklisted and imprisoned during the Red Scare of the 1960s.

Charles Butterworth was killed in a car wreck in Hollywood in 1946, bringing a premature close to his acting career after spending 20 years on Broadway and in Hollywood starring alongside Laurel and Hardy, Carole Lombard, Fred Astaire, Bob Hope, and Clark Gable. His death also brought an end to his engagement to actress Natalie Schafer, who would go on to be best known as Mrs. Howell in Gilligan's Island. He was honored with a star on the Hollywood Walk of Fame in 1960.

Dixie Dugan would remain in publication until 1966, but the strip outlasted both of its creators. McEvoy died in New York in 1958 and Striebel followed close behind in 1962.

Except Lardner, each of the News-Times superstars lasted well beyond the paper that launched them. The South Bend News-Times ended its publication run on December 27, 1938.

---

[12] According to his close friends, Lardner actually won a third Academy Award for a film he wrote under a pseudonym while he was blacklisted.

CHAPTER THIRTEEN
LIFESTYLES OF THE RICH AND THE FAMOUS (OF WILBER STREET)

Five years after his retirement from the big leagues, Babe Ruth returned to South Bend and brought with him the greatest collection of baseball talent that northern Indiana has ever seen. Ruth had made a good living playing ball, famously becoming the first professional athlete to make more than a sitting president, but quickly discovered that he could leverage his fame to make good money even after his playing days were over. For several years, Ruth crisscrossed the country with other big leaguers, making celebrity appearances and hosting high-powered baseball camps for youngsters new to the game.

That's what he'd come to do in June 1940, and with an impressive roster of all-time legends including future Hall of Famers in Rogers Hornsby and Dizzy Dean[13], Babe Ruth's Baseball Camp promised to be worth whatever price they asked.

Of course, there would also be the opportunity for the public to buy tickets to meet the players and to see an exhibition of their admittedly declining baseball skills. If it's at all possible, it seems that Ruth may not have been the biggest draw of the bunch. That honor might have belonged to another Hall of Famer and one-time Chicago Cubs manager, Rabbit Maranville.

As a shortstop, Maranville was known and lauded for his superb defense, a skill which boosted his standing in the league

---

[13] In addition to Hall of Famers in Ruth, Dean, and Hornsby; the camp also featured Hippo Vaughn, who claimed the pitching Triple Crown in 1918 for the Chicago Cubs. 1926 National League MVP, Bob O'Farrell was also part of the clinic. O'Farrell is most famous for being the catcher who threw out Babe Ruth to end the 1926 World Series days before Ruth's home run at Playland Park.

despite his pedestrian hitting numbers. He won a World Series with the Boston Braves in 1914 and for a long time, his 23 seasons in the National League were the record. As a reward for his long career, Rabbit Maranville retired with 2,605 hits.

But for all his accolades, Maranville's celebrity had little to do with his skill on the diamond and even less to do with his leadership acumen during his managing days. Instead, the slight middle infielder was famous for being the bawdiest practical joker in all the big leagues. For a public craving entertainment, Maranville wasn't a ballplayer.

He was a comedian.

Rabbit Maranville was legendary for his pranks, his hijinks, and his entrepreneurial showmanship. After his 1914 World Series victory, Maranville launched his own Vaudeville show, which included storytelling, singing, and the reenactment of major plays from the series. It was during one of those reenactments that Maranville slid off of the stage, into the orchestra pit, and onto a drum, leaving him with a broken leg.

As his career stretched into his 40s, Maranville found himself losing a step on the field and a tick in the batter's box, but as an entertainer, he was reaching toward ever-loftier heights. On the diamond, he adopted the peculiar habit of sitting on runners after he tagged them out, then posing as Rodin's *The Thinker*. Off the field, he went so far as to fake his own death in order to stage a prank on his teammates.

As player-manager for the Cubs in 1925, Maranville did not slow down, instituting just one rule with the team; that none of his players could fall asleep before he did and challenging them to see who could get by on the least amount of sleep. It was a curious managerial strategy and it didn't work out. The 1925 Cubs were among the worst teams in the history of franchise, but even the rumors of his imminent demise didn't bring pause to Maranville's screwy sense of humor. In his most macabre practical joke, Maranville posed as a paperboy barking the fictional news that the Cubs' manager had been fired. The joke became reality a day later.

But if South Bend fans were mad about Maranville's foibles with the National League club in nearby Chicago, they didn't show it when Rabbit came to town in 1940. In fact, the man's antics were given a billing roughly equal to the Babe's prodigious power:

Babe Ruth will be prevailed on for some long-distance practice hitting, and Maranville will do his comic didos, for which he is becoming more and more prominent all the time.

Organizers had been working behind the scenes for days and weeks to prep for the Babe's visit, scheduling activities and VIP meet-and-greets, cleaning up the baseball field, registering participants for the camp, and securing comfortable accomodations for the Bambino and his crew. This last part was no small task. Babe Ruth was more than just the greatest ballplayer in the history of the sport; he was also the most famous and recognizable man in America besides the President. He couldn't just lay his head *anywhere*. His lodging needed to suit his stature, and of course it did.

That's why they put him up at a house on Wilber Street.

It was a brick two-story just west of Portage Road and for a week in 1940 it was the palace of the Sultan of Swat, his wife, and his daughter. The place belonged to South Bend businessman

Dick Muessel who was happy to spend a week at his lakehouse so that the Ruths could have the home to themselves. And they would have too, except that when Dick Jr. laid eyes on Ruth's daughter, he came back twice during the week to mow a lawn that almost certainly did not need mowing.

The house is still there, well cared for and flanked by mature trees, and while there's nothing wrong with the place, it's difficult to imagine a time when Wilber Street would have been the chosen destination of the rich and the famous, crawling with early papparazzi hoping to get a picture of the nation's heroes. It's not that the press doesn't cover Wilber Street anymore. It's just that the coverage usually comes for far less savory reasons, and the headlines are rarely found on the society pages.

But in 1940, it might have been Topkapi Palace, at least for a time, and there was a buzz throughout South Bend as the city prepared for the Babe's arrival and for his scheduled hitting exhibitions at Lippincott Park. They remembered the last time that Ruth had come to town and hit a ball almost to the river. It would just take one swing of the bat for the man's legend to grow just a little bit more.

But it didn't happen.

Hampered by a leg injury and subpar stadium lighting, Ruth took several mighty swings during his showcase, but none of them left the yard. There would not be another souvenir bat made a gift to a child in the stands. A second planned hitting exhibition would be cancelled altogether, and his 1926 round-tripper at Playland Park would remain Ruth's only South Bend home run.

That's not to say that the trip was a complete bust. Even though he was a shadow of his former self on the diamond, Babe Ruth was still a formidable presence on the golf course, and in fact, from the moment he arrived in town, he was pressing reporters about the best place to play a round. The South Bend Country Club was already prepared for him. During a May 1940 meeting of club's Board of Directors, they passed a resolution:

It having come to the attention of Board that Herman (Babe) Ruth is to be in South Bend in the near future, it was decided to issue to him a guest card for one month, the same to permit him the use of the club without greens fee.

Ruth was quick to make use of the benefit afforded him and golfed a round with several South Bend businessmen, including Dick Muessel, whose house he was staying in. And while it doesn't quite compare to tracking down the mammoth bat that Ruth gifted to a young Tom Hoban back in 1926, it's still an impressive find to have the scorecard from the round[14], which Ruth won handily, written by Ruth's own hand:

Ruth filled his days while he was in town, but at the end of the night, once he'd enjoyed a round of golf, coached the kids at the diamond, and failed to impress during his exhibition, Ruth would retreat once again to his little palace on Wilber Street. Remarkably, he wasn't the first legend to rest his head in a bed on Wilber Street. He wouldn't be nearly the last one either.

---

[14] This chapter would not have been possible without contributions from Andy Nickle. Andy reached out to me to share pieces from his collection, including the image of this scorecard, the pullquote from the South Bend Country Club Board of Directors' minutes, and the anecdote about Dick Jr. mowing the lawn with an exuberant gusto while Ruth's family was in town.

Joe Montana spent a summer a half-mile south of the Bambino's South Bend castle, living above a local bar, and starring on the pub's softball team. Even Knute Rockne's first South Bend house was in this neighborhood, not more than a pair of Babe Ruth dingers away from the home of Dick Muessel.

And yet, somehow, Knute Rockne isn't even the most famous Rockne-adjacent figure to stay in a house in the Far Northwest neighborhood. Not by a longshot.

*   *   *

The summer of 1940 might have been the most exciting season in the history of South Bend, punctuated on either end by visits from some of the most impressive and noteworthy celebrities in the nation. June saw Babe Ruth and his collection of MVPs, Hall-of-Famers, and World Series champions. And then, as the summer wound to a close and the baseball season came to a halt alongside it, it was Hollywood's turn to steal the front page.

South Bend had been waiting with bated breath for the release of *Knute Rockne, All American* since the moment the film had been announced and the rumors of star-sightings began to spread throughout the town while scenes were filmed around Notre Dame. But the biggest news would come when they announced the premiere. Nowhere was Knute Rockne more hallowed than in St. Joseph County, and so it was only fitting – if somewhat atypical – that the film make its premiere in the heart of South Bend.

Knute Rockne, All American premiered on October 4 with simultaneous showings at four downtown South Bend theaters – the Grenada, the Colfax, the State, and the Palace. More than 100 journalists and celebrities turned out for the festivities, including Bob Hope, Pat O'Brien, and the Gipper himself, Ronald Reagan.

Celebrities walked a loop between the theaters, greeting fans and pausing for photos before stepping into the luxury boxes dressed up just for them in each of the theaters. An estimated 24,000 people crowded into downtown to rub shoulders with celebrities, even though there were not nearly enough theater seats for all of them to see the show. If South Bend has ever been rocking the way it was on this night, I'd love to see it.

Knute Rockne, All American opened strong and to favorable reviews; most notably for Reagan's performance, considered by many to be his finest work, and that includes his presidency.[15] The film was made with the blessing and input of Rockne's widow and

---

[15] Despite his status as a kind of cult hero in Michiana, Reagan was unable to make inroads within the staunchly Democratic South Bend city limits during either of his Presidential runs.

featured cameos by Rockne's friends and family. But most of all, it contained the line that made Reagan famous and would eventually become a part of his rallying cry on the campaign trail. It might be a violation of municipal law if I don't include it here:

I've got to go, Rock. It's all right. I'm not afraid. Some time, Rock, when the team is up against it, when things are wrong and the breaks are beating the boys, ask them to go in there with all they've got and win just one for the Gipper. I don't know where I'll be then, Rock. But I'll know about it, and I'll be happy.

In the film, Pat O'Brien's Rockne invokes the speech to propel his team toward a National Championship, but this is one case where reality is less romantic than fiction. Rockne's Gipper speech actually came during a pedestrian 5-4 season, but it did spur Notre Dame on toward victory over Army. Years later it would nudge Reagan into the most consequential Presidency of the second half of the 20th century.

Reagan would return to South Bend on a few occasions. During his Presidency, he was even a commencement speaker at Notre Dame. But perhaps none of his return visits were as interesting as a high-profile 1980 campaign stop in St. Joseph County. That's because, as his improbable political star was soaring toward impossibly new heights, Reagan and his wife needed a place in South Bend to stay the night, and so his team put him in the only place they could find that suited his stature.

They put him in a fine white house at the corner of Portage and Wilber Streets.

176

ACKNOWLEDGEMENTS

After I wrote my first book, <u>An Incomplete History of St. Joseph County, Indiana</u>; a lot of people asked me when I was going to write the sequel. For a long time, I wasn't sure I was going to. I thought it might be difficult to find the stories, but as it would turn out, the stories were going to find me.

I am indebted to great friends who delivered ideas and tales to me regularly; people like Bill Moor, Kirby Sprouls, Ken Bradford, Mike Wambaugh, Travis Childs, Andy Nickle, Paul Wasowski, Gabrielle Robinson, Garry Tutorow, Nimbi Cushing, Matt Meersman, Tim Hoban, and plenty more.

Of course, none of this book would have happened if the first book hadn't done so well, so thanks again to everyone who has supported my writing, who's stopped to say hello at fairs or conventions, or who's booked me to speak at their gatherings.

To Colton, Addy, Clara, and Olivia; thanks for always being a part of the adventure and always being willing to poke around through museums and cemeteries and old houses. To Ashley, thanks for going to Hell and back and everywhere else with me.

And for everyone who supported the Kickstarter campaign that made this book a reality, thanks for everything. This book is for you:

Ed Erickson	Dick Sullivan	Susan Cavallo
Larry Guy	Nimbi Cushing	Nancy Vandygriff
Kirk Robbins	Tyler Davis	Joan Shepherd
John McNamara	Paul Klockow	Greg Portolese
Scott Dunham	Matt Meersman	Kirby Sprouls
Barb Carmichael	Doug Fecher	Debi Shertzer
Andrew Martin	Nora Zusi	Spike Abernathy

Brad Citter	Warren Williams	Paul Woods
Laura McCann	Ken Bradford	Mike Reichmann
Lukus	Bill Moor	Carla Fay
Regina Emberton	Tabitha Butts	Brian McClintock
Terry	Shari Baker	Luke Clark
Mary Latowski	Mike Bieganski	Josh Crabill
Martha Alsio	Patricia Davis	John Sovinski
Peggy Henderson	Mike & Julie Helman	Leila Cook
Frank Perri	Ross	Jacob Kisor
Dan Erickson	Tom Kuzmic	Eleanor Boothman
Nate Steward	Lisa Mercado	Jared Rensberger

ABOUT THE AUTHOR

Aaron Helman is a historian, adventurer, and humorist from South Bend, Indiana. He is the author of <u>An Incomplete History of St. Joseph County, Indiana</u>, <u>Simon Rousseau and the House on the Hill</u>, and <u>First, Get a Million Dollars</u>.

He is a contributor at <u>moorandmore.net</u>, a long-distance cyclist, and can often be spotted eating tacos. Follow Aaron's work and order copies of his books at **aaronhelman.com**.